Expeditions
Unpacked

What the Great Explorers
Took into the Unknown

Expeditions

Unpacked

 WHITE LION
PUBLISHING

ED STAFFORD

Contents

Opposite Geologist Thomas Griffith Taylor and meteorologist Charles Wright in the entrance to an ice grotto during Captain Robert Falcon Scott's 'Terra Nova' Expedition to the Antarctic, 5 January 1911.

Introduction

If the secret world of expeditions is locked behind a huge oak door for most of us, then equipment is the key that will grant us access. Sure, we need to know how to deftly turn that key, but the difference between thriving in Arkansas or the Arctic is largely down to the kit we choose to take with us.

In a lofty realm of visions, records and world-firsts, it's often hard to pin down exactly what makes an expedition an expedition. Is it danger, moral courage or dogged determination? By it's very nature, it's ethereal. Whereas solid objects are tangible and real – we can prod them and analyse them while we ponder these bigger questions. Perhaps they give us an insight into the explorer, their motives and mind. Perhaps they tell us something about their character that will challenge our own concepts of how we should live our lives.

If you've grown up geeking-out on equipment as I have, then, as you enter this world of expeditions, you may feel a strong urge to buy the very latest

and best items available. Surely it's the kit that enables you to climb higher and run further, right?

When I first led an expedition to Argentine Patagonia I knew that it was going to be chilly (not Chile), so I purchased enough Antarctic sleeping bags and down jackets that if I'd stayed at home and flogged them on eBay could have raised a deposit for a small house. I obsessed over fabrics and technical details so much that, after one particularly unromantic night spent arguing about the properties of three-ply Gore tex, my partner left me.

The phrase 'all the gear but no idea' was stuck to me with gaffer tape. But it was a necessarily awkward internship into a work arena that I now know and love. Today, as a grizzly forty-something, I take huge pleasure from embarking on an adventure without that level of preparation. Knowing that I can handle a situation without all the gadgets gives me a deep sense of confidence. Whether it's wearing barefoot trainers up Ben Nevis or being deliberately stranded on a tropical

EXPEDITIONS UNPACKED

Left In February 2018, three female adventurers, led by the British explorer Laura Bingham, become the first team to navigate the entire length of the Essequibo River.

island for sixty days naked, knowing that I can cope, irrespective of what I have to hand, is as reassuring as the silhouette of a Land Rover at the end of weeks of trekking.

But clearly, in most cases, it's a balance. We need enough kit to keep us alive and relatively comfortable, but not so much that we are heavily burdened and therefore miserable. Careful selection of exactly the right equipment to get a job done is what we are working towards. If it doesn't have a vital purpose then it's not coming 'just in case'. Or perhaps it is … Once you're experienced enough, you might decide you can afford to absorb that luxurious handicap of taking an accordion into the Amazon rainforest as Percy Fawcett did on his expedition to discover the Lost City of Z.

To see the lists of kit in the pages of this book gives an insight into the explorer and how they think. How meticulous were they? How experienced? How amusingly blasé?

The final entry in this book is a world-first river descent led by Laura Bingham (see page 224). The night before they were due to take a twin-propeller Cessna deep into the remote Guyanese jungle, Bingham's expedition partner and room-mate, Ness Knight, meticulously laid out all of her kit on her bed. Knight needed the mental clarity that she had everything and knew where everything was before she packed it away – something I completely get. Bingham (who happens also to be my lunatic wife) came in and, as a joke, pulled away the bed covers to tip all of the kit into a heap on the floor. Somehow the two continue to be the best of friends having subsequently kayaked the entire Essequibo together, but I know that I would have exploded if she'd done that to me. Bingham's intention was to cut the pre-expedition tension I know – she just wanted everyone to laugh – but, when you play with someone else's kit, you are playing with fire.

Sometimes, a piece of kit comes along that enables a complete re-evaluation of what is physically possible and it's very exciting. In 2006, I was introduced to the inflatable packraft in Patagonia. I immediately saw the versatility of this craft and an old dream expedition of mine started bubbling to the surface. I'd dreamed about walking the length of the Amazon River for years but always drew a blank when it came to crossing the hundreds of tributaries. There were simply too many, they were too fast-flowing to swim with all my kit and building a raft every time with a machete was a ridiculous concept. Suddenly, technology evolved, and here was a boat that packed down to the size of an old sleeping mat and didn't weigh much more. With carbon-fibre four-piece split paddles it meant I could cross any water body in my path. A previously impossible journey could now be attempted (see page 170).

On the same expedition, a very different piece of kit also revolutionised the trip. About a year into the walk, I ran out of money. Without it I could no longer buy food, pay for insurance, hire local guides or afford website maintenance. In days gone by, I would have had to hold my hands up and admit defeat – expedition over. But on this trip I was carrying a BGAN (satellite Internet link). I uploaded a video, cut to a Coldplay soundtrack (for maximum tugging of heartstrings) and put a Paypal link next to it asking people to help fund the expedition. The response was extraordinary and

over the course of the next year, the video raised over £40,000. To be able to communicate with the outside world from the depths of the Amazon saved my expedition – and enabled me to achieve a Guinness World Record.

But as much as I admire the theodolites and sextants, the oilskins and the water drums, it's the frivolous items that I find myself drawn to. Sir Robin Knox-Johnston sailed around the world with Tennent's Lager, whisky and Bovril, whereas Jason Lewis pedalled, rowed and paddled across oceans with Castle Eden Ale, whisky (again) and Marmite. But can we even call these items whimsical? On the face of it, it's not too hard to imagine that the gruelling days and nights would have been impossible to survive without a nightcap and a tiny slice of home. But digging deeper, perhaps the very items that make me grin are the ones that reveal a mischievous character: 'It's my expedition and I'll take what I bloody want!' And why not? Could it be that this two-fingered salute to common sense is in fact the bolshy character trait that made the expedition happen in the first place?

From accordions to pianos, canines to camels, the mix of essentials and extraordinaries over the centuries has been fascinating to research and write about in a manner that lays bare these explorers' remarkable minds. Whether you read it from cover to cover or simply dip into it on a coffee break, I sincerely hope that I've managed to capture the sense of wonder at these astounding feats of human endeavour and how each explorer's own personal kit selection helps us to get inside the minds of those who have chosen a life less ordinary.

Expeditions

Nellie Bly

Born: 5 May 1864, USA
Died: 27 January 1922, USA

Nellie Bly was the pen name for Elizabeth Cochrane, a trailblazing journalist who rose through the ranks of the male-dominated American media to become a star reporter with the *New York World*. One Sunday evening in the winter of 1888, struck down with writer's block, Bly wished that she were: 'At the other end of the Earth!' This was the lightbulb moment that led her to attempt a record-breaking feat: to circumnavigate the globe faster than Jules Verne's hero from the novel *Around the World in Eighty Days*.

Round the World Unpacked

Expedition:
Round the world

Date:
1889–1890

Length:
72 days

1. Travel coat (Scotch Ulster)
2. Special Passport No. 247
3. Underwear
4. Mumm champagne
5. Slippers
6. Twenty-dollar gold pieces
7. Silk bodice
8. Handkerchief
9. Small flask and drinking cup
10. Jar of cold cream
11. McGinty the monkey
12. Travelling dress
13. British gold sovereigns
14. Veils
15. Ink stand
16. Pens and pencils
17. Dark gloves
18. Travelling caps
19. Tennis blazer
20. Toilet articles
21. Hairbrush
22. Dressing gown
23. Copy paper
24. Pins, needles and thread
25. Brown leather gripsack
26. Silk waterproof wrap

Nellie Bly had a fearsome reputation as a dogged investigative journalist; aged just twenty, she had spent ten days undercover in the Women's Lunatic Asylum on Blackwell's Island, exposing the brutal treatment of patients, which led to widespread reforms in care for the mentally ill. So, when Bly explained her plan, to beat Phileas Fogg's fictional globetrotting record, she was a little shocked by her editor's response: 'You would need a protector, and … you would need so much baggage that it would detain you in making rapid changes. Besides, you speak nothing but English, so there is no use talking about it; no one but a man can do this.' Bly's reply soon changed his mind: 'Very well. Start the man and I'll start the same day for some other newspaper and beat him.' Bly was a force of nature; he couldn't afford to lose her.

The newspaper sat on the idea for almost a year, and then gave Bly just two days' notice before she would board the *Augusta Victoria* bound for Southampton, England, and begin her round-the-world challenge.

Bly knew that the key to her success would be to take no more with her than she could squeeze into her brown leather gripsack, to avoid delays with lost luggage or bureaucratic customs officials; a strategy, no doubt, inspired by the light-travelling Phileas Fogg and his famous carpet bag.

Bly set off for the fashionable part of New York to visit one of the city's most prestigious dressmakers, William Ghormley of Fifth Avenue.

'I want a dress that will stand constant wear for three months,' she explained, adding that it needed to be ready by that very evening, rather than the usual seven-day turnaround. Ghormley, who was used to dealing with the country's wealthiest and most demanding clients, was unfazed.

They settled on a blue broadcloth and a patterned camel's-hair as the most suitable fabrics for a durable travelling gown. In other shops she bought dark gloves, a long black-and-white plaid Scotch Ulster (a heavy-duty woollen overcoat with a cape and sleeves) to keep out the cold and a lightweight summer dress for warmer climes – which she ultimately had to sacrifice in favour of 'last summer's silk bodice' due to space.

As she noted in her journal: 'One never knows the capacity of an ordinary hand-satchel until dire necessity compels the exercise … in mine I was able to pack two travelling caps, three veils, a pair of slippers, a complete outfit of toilet articles, ink-stand, pens, pencils, and copy paper.' These last few items were vitally important, since Bly would be posting letters from every port of call so that the *New York World* could serialise her exploits.

'Pins, needles and thread,' were also packed, to keep her limited wardrobe in one piece, along with: 'a dressing gown, a tennis blazer, a small flask and a drinking cup, several complete changes of underwear, a liberal supply of handkerchiefs and fresh ruchings.' The only luxury item she noted was: 'a jar of cold cream to keep my face from chapping in the varied climates I should encounter.' Barely able to close the bag's clasp, she resorted to carrying her silk waterproof wrap over her arm.

Just five hours before she was about to set sail, with a little help from the US Secretary of State, Special Passport No. 247 was delivered to the Hoboken docks, where staff from the *World* were busy making last-minute checks to Bly's travel plans.

Unbeknown to Bly and her colleagues, among the hustle and bustle of Hoboken harbour that morning, a man called John Brisben Walker, publisher of *The Cosmopolitan* magazine, was busy scanning over Bly's itinerary, which the *New York World* had proudly splashed over its front pages.

Walker, who never missed the opportunity to increase his readership, immediately decided to race one of his own reporters around the world to grab the glory for themselves.

As Bly set out for England, aboard the steamship *Augusta Victoria*, at 9.40 a.m. on Thursday, 14 November 1889, little did she know that just six

NELLIE BLY

hours later, Elizabeth Bisland, a twenty-eight-year-old literary editor with *The Cosmopolitan*, would board a Central Line train, heading west for San Francisco, beginning her race around the globe in the opposite direction.

Bly had never taken a sea voyage before, and she was stricken with violent seasickness, running to the rail to 'vent' for most of that first day. 'And she's going around the world!' joked one passenger, which even Bly found funny, when she considered that land was barely out of sight and 32,000km (22,000 miles) of mostly ocean lay ahead. By the time she found her sea legs they had docked in Southampton, arriving just in time to pick up the late-night mail train to London and her connections over the Channel and on towards Paris.

Despite her gruelling schedule, Bly took a short detour to Amiens to meet Jules Verne and his wife. This was the celebrated author who had inspired her whole adventure; how could she refuse? In his grand house Bly spent a pleasant evening comparing her intended route with the framed world map that hung in Verne's hallway, where a thin blue line marked out Fogg's travels from the best-selling novel. Bly found the Vernes to be a charming couple but secretly suspected that Verne doubted the trip could be done in less than eighty days. 'If you do it in seventy-nine days, I shall applaud with both hands,' he said.

The journey through France and over the Italian border was cold and uncomfortable. Just the previous week, in this remote part of northern Italy, the train had been attacked by bandits; Bly half-hoped they would strike again: 'If the passengers then felt the scarcity of blankets, they at least had some excitement to make their blood circulate.' For this reason some of her colleagues had urged her to pack a revolver as a 'companion piece' for the Special Passport. But Bly decided against it, declaring that: 'I had such a strong belief in the world's greeting me as I greeted it, that I refused to arm myself.'

Eleven days after leaving New York, Bly arrived in the port of Brindisi, on the heel of Italy, just in time to join a P&O steamer bound for Ceylon (now Sri Lanka).

Due to her lack of luggage a rumour had spread among the passengers that Miss Bly was an eccentric heiress, travelling with no more than a 'hairbrush and a bank book'. This led to quite a bit of unwanted attention from the eligible young bachelors on board, including one well-travelled chap who declared his admiration, adding that he: 'never expected to find a woman who could travel without a number of trunks and bundles innumerable.' When Bly asked him how many trunks the dapper young gentleman carried himself, 'nineteen' was the reply.

After leaving Port Said, Egypt, and passing through the Suez Canal, the *Oriental* anchored in the palm-fringed bay at Colombo, Ceylon, on 8 December 1889. Bly might not have been a millionaire heiress, as some had suspected, but she did carry £200 in British gold sovereigns and Bank of England notes, plus a smaller sum of American gold and currency; the notes she kept in a chamois-skin bag tied around her neck while the gold was buried deep in her pockets.

Aboard the steamship *Oriental*, Bly pressed onwards to Penang in British Malaya (now part of Malaysia) and into the Straits of Malacca. During an eleven-hour stop in Singapore, Bly visited the markets and fell in love with a little brown monkey, that she bought on the assurance of the seller that he was quite tame. Back on board the *Oriental*, on the long and rough voyage to Hong Kong, the monkey didn't enamour himself to his fellow passengers. McGinty, as he was christened, proved to be a bad-tempered little fellow, and a 'bit of a biter', especially when he was hungover. One day, after some men had been 'toasting its health', Bly found the monkey: 'holding its aching head … and, evidently thinking I was the cause of the swelling, it sprang at me.'

Bly was able to send short telegraphs to keep the *World* informed of her progress from the port offices where she docked. It was in the Hong Kong offices of the Occidental & Oriental Steamship Company that Bly finally learned of her rival from *The Cosmopolitan*. To make matters worse, Bly heard rumours that its editor had given Bisland a blank chequebook to bribe ships' captains to set sail ahead of schedule. Refusing to be downhearted, Bly figured her fate was out of her hands; she would stick to her plans and press on regardless.

Aboard the *Oceanic*, Bly's last port of call was Yokohama, Japan, before the final 7,300km (4,525-mile) shlep across the Pacific back to California. The *Oceanic*'s crew were determined to deliver her home ahead of schedule despite the poor weather; down in the engine room the chief engineer had even scrawled the couplet 'For Nellie Bly, we'll win or die' across the boilers to motivate the stokers.

Despite the crew's best efforts, storms at sea put them two days behind schedule. However, as Bly was being ferried ashore in California, she learnt that her rival, Bisland, had missed her fast German steamer back to New York and was still stuck at sea on the *Bothnia*, one of the slowest ships in the transatlantic fleet. It seemed that the race was still on.

In the port of San Francisco the customs and quarantine officials sat up all night to make their cursory checks and speed her on her way before a specially chartered train, laid on by the *World*'s owner, Joseph Pulitzer, whisked Bly overland on her final leg back to New York.

The crowds erupted as the *Miss Nellie Bly Special* steamed away on its journey east. Despite slowing down occasionally, so Bly could wave her cap at various stations en route (and present bottles of Mumm champagne to the railways' superintendents who had fast-tracked her passage), the train made record time, pulling into New Jersey train station on 25 January 1890, at 3.51 p.m.

As she stepped onto the platform thousands of waving onlookers let out a deafening cheer, cannons were fired and vessels in the harbour sounded their hooters and whistles, in salute to Bly, the female adventurer who had 'girdled the world' in just seventy-two days and enraptured the nation.

Captain Robert Falcon Scott

Born: 6 June 1868, UK
Died: 29 March 1912, Antarctica

Robert Falcon Scott first set to sea as a Royal Navy midshipman in 1883 aged just thirteen years old. Rising quickly through the ranks, he eventually attracted the attention of the Royal Geographical Society, which put him in command of the 1901 National Antarctic 'Discovery' Expedition. When Scott successfully returned to England in 1904, having travelled further south than anyone before, he was hailed as a national hero. Utterly captivated by this little-known continent, in 1910 he left on the *Terra Nova:* 'To reach the South Pole, and to secure for the British Empire the honour of this achievement.'

Race to the Pole Unpacked

Expedition:
Race to the Pole

Date:
1910–1912

Length:
1 year 4 months

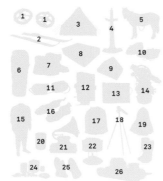

1. Pony snowshoes
2. Skis
3. Tents
4. Pendulum inclinometer
5. Ponies
6. Reindeer skin sleeping bag
7. Finnesko
8. Fry's chocolate
9. Artificial horizon
10. Steel crampons
11. Goggles
12. Camera
13. Book bag
14. Theodolite
15. Clothing
16. Ski overshoes
17. Knitted woollen underwear
18. Telescope
19. Burberry gabardine jacket
20. Heinz baked beans
21. HMV gramophone
22. Camping stove
23. Leather overshoes
24. Food rations
25. Wolfskin mittens
26. Motor sled

Right The *Terra Nova* moored to the ice sheet in the Ross Dependency, during Captain Robert Falcon Scott's second expedition to the Antarctic – January 1911.

Robert Falcon Scott's expedition to the Antarctic began in Cardiff Bay, Wales, aboard the *Terra Nova*. He arrived in Melbourne, Australia, in October 1910, to collect crew and supplies. While here, Scott received a telegram from Norwegian explorer Roald Amundsen: 'Beg leave to inform you *Fram* proceeding Antarctic'. Amundsen wasn't giving much away, but it seemed the expedition had become a race.

Despite Scott's bravado, the *Terra Nova* venture had never intended to be an all-out 'Pole-hunt'.

Eight thousand people had applied to join the sixty-five-man expedition, and from that number twelve eminent scientists had been selected to study Antarctica's unique biology, geology, glaciology and meteorology. On board the *Terra Nova* were boxes of high-tech apparatus including telescopes, deep-water sampling devices, hypsometers, thermometers and pendulum inclinometers for accurate cartographic surveying. Much of this scientific equipment had been adapted for polar exploration, including Scott's tripod-mounted theodolite, which he used to calculate longitude and latitude. This had been fitted with leather gaskets around its knobs and eyepiece to prevent frostbite on contact with skin.

The *Terra Nova* reached the Ross Ice Shelf in January 1911. To help with the heavy hauling from the ship, and the laying of supply depots ahead of the main expedition, Scott had acquired three caterpillar-tracked motor sledges. Custom-built for the expedition, each one of these experimental vehicles cost more than a Rolls-Royce, and many believed that they would give Scott's team the technological advantage over his Norwegian rivals.

Unfortunately, one crashed through the pack ice while being unloaded, sinking sixty fathoms into the icy depths. Scott (who was quietly sceptical about the motor sledges' reliability) also brought along thirty-three sledging dogs and nineteen Mongolian ponies – sadly, two ponies also fell through the pack ice during unloading and were eaten by killer wales.

Ponies had served Scott well on previous expeditions, and special snowshoes had been designed for this adventure made from wire and bamboo with leather fastening straps. However, only one Pony, Weary Willie, was fitted with them, a mistake that severely hindered their progress over soft ground.

The two remaining motor sledges had proved useful shuttling supplies from the *Terra Nova*

to base camp, but in the drifting snow heading south they were pretty useless. They frequently overheated in the dry polar air, had a top speed of just three miles per hour and much of their payload was taken up with the fuel required to run them. When they finally broke down, just days into the Southern Party's trek towards the Pole, they were simply abandoned.

Scott's plan was to have just two ponies remaining when they reached the base of the Beardmore Glacier. The others would be shot along the way and their meat consumed by the men and dogs. The team hated killing their ponies, after they had served so well pulling 450lb (200kg) loads on sledges made of wood, leather and rope. In their diaries they recorded that the animals had 'died of old age precipitated by a bullet'.

The dog teams impressed Scott greatly. He noted that they: 'were doing well and pulling 800lb' (360kg). However, Scott had underestimated their food needs, and with dwindling supplies he reluctantly sent them back to base camp, while the remaining team set off to man-haul the sledges up the Beardmore Glacier.

The last of the ponies were shot when the team reached Shambles Camp, on 9 December 1911.

In his diaries Scott noted that five members of the Southern Party were now suffering from 'snow blindness due to incaution'. Most men wore goggles with smoked glass lenses, but these were prone to frosting over, and when the men removed them for any period the sunlight reflecting off the bright white snow would singe their corneas causing immense pain. 'The alternatives were to have a piece of leather with a slit in place of the glass or to have goggles cut from a piece of wood.'

While the Norwegian's favoured Inuit-style fur coats and long wolfskin boots, Scott felt that this would be too warm and bulky for a largely man-powered expedition on foot. His team wore Burberry gabardine jackets, which were lightweight, waterproof and windproof. However, the tightly woven fabric did not breathe well, which caused the underlying layers of clothing to become sodden with sweat as they laboured with their sledges. Unable to adjust these layers in their cumbersome wolfskin mittens, their wet clothing soon lost its insulating properties. The jacket's lack of integrated hood also left the neck exposed, chilling the men even further.

Many brands were keen to sell, or in many cases donate, their wares to these heroic polar explorers.

In addition to Burberry, many other well-known brands supplied clothing to Scott's team, including Wolsey thermal baselayers and Jaeger woollen wear. Before the *Terra Nova* set sail the crew were also gifted 35,000 cigars, boxes of Fry's chocolate, Heinz baked beans, Huntley & Palmers' 'sledging biscuits' and an HMV gramophone. The Bass brewery even donated some crates of King's Ale, which they hoped Scott would drink to toast the King's health when he reached the South Pole.

Newman and Guardia in London custom-made lightweight cameras for the sledging parties to take with them. Although the explorers were novice photographers, they documented their adventures right until the end, taking photographs of unusual geological formations as part of their scientific research, and action shots of the men stumbling through the knee-high snowdrifts anchored to their single sledge.

On 20 December 1911, as the men rested, Scott selected the four-man team of Edward Wilson, Henry Bowers, Lawrence Oates and Edgar Evans, to join him on the final push for the Pole, 970km (600 miles) to the south. A bitterly

Below Stacking supplies at Cape Evans on Ross Island, 23 January 1911. Antarctica's most active volcano, Mount Erebus, is visible in the background.

cold wind battered the two tents, as they tried desperately to keep warm that night.

The tents, made from a green Willesden canvas, were lined to provide insulation and supported on six bamboo poles to form a pyramid shape about nine-feet square. This simple yet effective design would continue to be used by polar explorers for the next seventy years.

The expedition's reindeer skin sleeping bags had initially performed well, but out on the ice they became wet and bulky, more than doubling in weight. At night the men would have to prise the half-frozen layers apart. 'If we were fortunate, we became warm enough during the night to thaw the ice … and soon both were sheets of armour-plate,' wrote one team member.

When trekking on hard ice the men put on their steel crampons to gain purchase, but when they

approached drifting snow, as they did on Christmas day 1911, they found it easier to haul their sledges on skis. Fifty pairs of hickory wood skis had been purchased from Oslo and a young Norwegian ski instructor had been brought along on the *Terra Nova* to teach Scott's men the basics. Hauling 90kg (200lb) sledges on foot or ski was an exhausting task and the men were burning up around 7,000 calories a day. However, they were only consuming just over 4,000 calories, from a diet that was also lacking in Vitamin C and essential fats. Rations generally consisted of dried biscuits, chocolate, raisins, pemmican (ground meat mixed with animal fat) supplemented with horsemeat. With such a large calorie deficit the men were rapidly losing weight and scurvy was becoming a real threat.

By 15 January 1912, just 43km (27 miles) from the Pole, the weather began to deteriorate, with

night-time temperatures falling to -28°C (-18°F). Nevertheless, Scott's diary remained upbeat.

However, on 16 January 1912, that was to change. Lieutenant Bowers spotted a black speck in the far distance. 'We marched on, found that it was a black flag tied to a sledge bearer; nearby the remains of a camp; sledge tracks and ski tracks going and coming; and the clear trace of dogs' paws. This told us the whole story. The Norwegians have forestalled us and are first at the Pole.'

Continuing on and arriving at the South Pole the next day, they planted their 'poor slighted Union Jack' in front of the Norwegian flag left by Amundsen, and, using a long thread to release the shutter, took a poignant final photograph of the despondent Southern Party.

'Great God! This is an awful place,' wrote Scott in his diary that evening. 'We have turned our back now on the goal of our ambition and must face our 800 miles of solid dragging.'

For almost a month the five-man team battled biting polar winds, drifting snow and night-time temperatures approaching -40°C (-40°F). With an energy deficit of 3,000 calories per day the men had lost around 25kg (55lb) in body fat and muscle mass making it impossible to keep warm. Edgar Evans was the first to succumb to exhaustion: collapsing on the perilous descent of the Beardmore Glacier he hit his head, dying of a suspected brain haemorrhage at the glacier's foot.

The remaining four battled northwards making camp at supply depots they had set up on the way as they found them. At each one they discovered much of their cooking fuel had evaporated – the leather washers that sealed the fuel canisters had failed in the severe cold – making it impossible

Above left Geologist Frank Debenham grinds stone samples at base camp in the Ross Dependency of Antarctica, 12 July 1911.

Above right Captain Robert Falcon Scott, leader of the 1910 British Antarctic Expedition, wearing his finnesko boots, wolfskin mittens and Burberry gabardine jacket.

to heat quantities of food or melt enough ice for drinking water.

By March, Captain Oates began to suffer the agonising effects of frostbite in his feet. He could no longer assist with sledge-pulling duties and the party's progress slowed considerably.

Soft finnesko boots had been made by the Sami people of northern Finland for the British expedition, constructed of reindeer fur, lined with felt and insulated with dried leaves from a type of sedge called sennegrass. While this footwear could be very effective (especially in conjunction with a leather overshoe that skis or crampons could be attached to), there was some skill required in repacking the shoes as the sennegrass broke down. As Scott noted: 'Although we all tried to imitate the Finns in their skill at this work, none of us felt as warm on our feet as when they had helped us.'

As the finnesko lost their insulation, Oates' feet became blackened by frostbite and gangrene set in. Knowing that his condition was becoming a burden, Oates announced to his tent-mates on the night of 17 March 1912: 'I am just going outside and may be sometime.' He walked out into a -40°C (-40°F) blizzard and certain death.

Scott, Wilson and Bowers soldiered on for another three days, trudging a further 32km (20 miles) north, before they were halted by ferocious snowstorms. Trapped in their tent for nine days, too weak and cold to advance any further, Scott recorded his final diary entry on 29 March 1912: 'The end cannot be far. It seems a pity but I do not think I can write more ... For God's sake look after our people.'

Ultimately, it was a combination of bad luck, appalling weather and deficiencies in equipment that led to Scott's defeat and the loss of his men. However, unlike Amundsen's, the *Terra Nova* expedition was also a scientific undertaking; a mission that even in their darkest hours the five-man southern party never abandoned. Measurements of how magnetic fields wavered at the Pole were recorded, meteorological data was meticulously logged and when Scott's body was eventually recovered they discovered 16kg (35lb) of rock samples still packed away in his sledge – some of which contained fossils that would later be used to develop the theory of plate tectonics.

Scott might have lost the race, but as he once said: 'It is the work that matters, not the applause that follows.'

EXPEDITIONS UNPACKED

Above Scott's team pose by the partially collapsed tent of Roald Amundsen, 18 January 1912; the Norwegian explorers had beaten the British to the South Pole by almost a month.

Roald Amundsen

Born: 16 July 1872, Norway

Disappeared: June 1928, Barents Sea

As a young man Roald Amundsen was inspired by the great Norwegian explorer Fridtjof Nansen, who, in 1895, had made an unsuccessful attempt to reach the North Pole in the *Fram* – a 39m (128ft), three-masted schooner which was purpose-built for Arctic exploration. Clad in the sturdy timber of the South American greenheart tree, it was reinforced to withstand enormous pressure and had a shallow rounded hull to ride out of frozen pack ice. In 1908, Amundsen obtained the blessing of the Norwegian Geographical Society for his own attempt on the Pole and was given a 75,000 kroner grant to refit the *Fram* for its long journey north.

Race to the Pole
Unpacked

Expedition:
Race to the Pole

Date:
1910–1912

Length:
1 year 7 months

1. Mandolin
2. Books
3. Piano
4. Norwegian pemmican
5. Amundsen-designed ski boots
6. Skis
7. Sextants
8. The Norwegian flag
9. Compass
10. Amundsen's biscuits
11. Snow knives
12. Records
13. Artifical horizon
14. Snowshoes
15. Clothing
16. Primus stove
17. Sledge meter
18. Mittens
19. Lightweight assault sledges
20. Gramophone
21. Greenland dogs
22. Violin
23. Fram

Roald Amundsen's preparations for his assault on the North Pole were going well. He knew from bitter experience that crews caught up in drifting pack ice could quickly become demoralised. So, to combat boredom, he had the *Fram* fitted out with a library containing 3,000 books and a gramophone with a broad selection of records. There was also a range of musical instruments on board, including a piano, a violin, some mandolins and sheet music donated by their Norwegian sponsors.

However, in September 1909 newspapers reported that the American explorer Robert E. Peary had become the first man to reach the North Pole. A frustrated Amundsen quickly realised that this news would diminish public interest in his own Arctic adventures: 'If I was now to succeed in arousing interest in my undertaking, there was nothing left for me but to try to solve the last great problem – the South Pole.'

At first Amundsen kept this change of plan to himself. In his memoirs he claimed not to have felt any great scruples with regard to other Antarctic expeditions that were being planned at the time. 'The British expedition was designed entirely for scientific research. The Pole was only a side-issue,' he wrote.

Nevertheless, he felt he should telegraph Captain Scott of his intentions as a 'mark of courtesy'. Back in Britain the Royal Geographical Society and other supporters of the *Terra Nova* expedition didn't see things quite the same way.

The *Fram* left Oslo on 7 June 1910, bound for the Portuguese island of Madeira 480km (300 miles) off the North African coast, to pick up supplies of explosives and ammunition. It was here, several weeks after setting off, that Amundsen told his nineteen-man crew of their new objective.

On board, among the mountains of provisions that had been methodically catalogued and stowed, were four hundred bundles of dried fish, two hundred felt blankets, ninety-seven dogs and a canary called Fridtjof. When they reached the Bay of Whales, off the Ross Ice Shelf, six months later, the number of dogs had increased to 116.

Like the British, the first order of business was to erect a prefabricated hut, from where preparations for depot laying, ahead of the final assault, would be made.

Over the long polar winter, at their 'Framheim' (home of the *Fram*) base camp, 200 seals were butchered for the shore party and their dog teams. Amundsen had learned from his previous adventures that fresh lightly cooked meat was a good source of Vitamin C and offered protection against scurvy.

Olav Bjaaland, a champion skier and talented carpenter, got to work improving the expedition sledges, reducing their weight to almost a third by planing down their frames and runners, and constructing new lightweight assault sledges, from surplus hickory wood, for the final push across the polar plateau.

Unlike Scott's off-the-shelf sport skis, Amundsen's team were equipped with custom-made extra-long versions that reduced the chances of slipping into a crevasse. The Norwegians' tents were also very different, constructed of lightweight wind cloth (dyed black with shoe polish to soak up the sun's heat) with built-in floors and erected by a single pole. For cooking Amundsen selected the Swedish-designed Primus stove that had already proved itself on Nansen's Arctic expedition.

Over the winter nearly 3.5 tonnes of supplies were laid at three main depots along their intended route to the South Pole. Clothing and equipment were constantly evaluated with each man taking responsibility for modifying their Amundsen-designed ski boots to avoid blisters and frostbite.

At the first hint of spring in October 1911 five men, four sledges and fifty-two dogs began their dash for the Pole. Three of the sledges had steel

Right Amundsen liked to keep his crew busy. Here the Norwegians are fabricating leather goods which included Eskimo-style suits and nose protectors for their sunglasses.

fittings and were fitted with sledge meters, made from a bicycle wheel that logged each revolution. The other one, that carried the compass, was built mostly from aluminium. Packed on each were 300kg (668lb) of provisions and a personal bag, in which they kept clothing and observation journals. Each man also carried a watch (which was needed for navigation) and a double-layered sleeping bag. Rather than the heavy trunks that Scott's men carried, these items were stashed in compressible waxed cotton 'pulk' bags.

Amundsen firmly believed that his use of dogs, rather than ponies, would be the deciding factor in the success of his mission. His husky-like Greenland dogs were adapted to the cold climate with small fur-covered ears that reduced the chance of frostbite. As working dogs, they were prized

more for their strength and stamina than their temperament. Scott's ponies might have been more placid, but they perspired when worked hard and needed blanketing to avoid hypothermia. They also required their own fodder, while dogs could eat the same rations as the men – seal and penguin meat, or, ultimately, each other.

Amundsen was to adopt a dog-eat-dog fuelling strategy as they neared the Pole, whereby the weaker dogs would be butchered and fed to the others, using a formula that Amundsen had devised relating pulling power to sledge weights. Many of Scott's men were slightly horrified by this canine cannibalism, but, strangely, had less qualms about eating their own ponies.

On 17 November 1911, with a depleted team of forty-two sledge dogs, the expedition reached the

EXPEDITIONS UNPACKED

Transatlantic Mountain. After some searching they found a path upwards along a steep glacier that ascended 3,230m (10,600ft) to the polar plateau above. After four days of hard climbing they reached the top where they repacked supplies on to three sledges that would be pulled by only eighteen of the fittest remaining dogs. Each sledge-driver now faced the grim task of slaughtering the surplus animals from their teams. 'We called the place the Butchers' Shop,' Amundsen noted. 'The holiday humour that ought to have prevailed in the tent that evening – our first on the plateau – did not make its appearance; there was depression and sadness in the air – we had grown so fond of our dogs.'

Fog and bad weather waylaid their departure for several days and made it difficult for Amundsen to get an accurate fix on their location using their sextants. Although these were lighter and less cumbersome than Scott's theodolite, sextants were primarily designed for use at sea where readings were taken relative to the horizon. This required the Norwegians to use an artificial horizon made from a tray of mercury. The angles recorded were then compared to that year's Nautical Almanac, a table of data that gave you your precise latitude and longitude. Uncharacteristically, Amundsen had forgotten to bring the 1912 almanac; if they were to locate the South Pole they would have to do so before the end of 1911.

After a hard few weeks traversing an area of deadly hidden crevasses, christened The Devil's Ballroo', they made camp within striking distance of their goal on 12 December 1911. Waking the next morning, having temporarily lost his bearings,

With the sledges, dogs tethered to a long line to avoid in-fighting, Amundsen's team stash their skis to make camp for the night.

Amundsen was shocked to see an unusual black dot on the horizon. Fearing that the Brits had beaten him to it, he was relieved to discover that it was only a pile of his own dogs' faeces, magnified by a mirage.

By 14 December 1911 they knew they were getting close and spent the next three days trying to get an accurate fix on the Pole using sextants and their sledge meters. On 17 December 1911, Amundsen's men came to a consensus and pitched a small tent at the South Pole, in which they stowed surplus food and equipment, and a letter to the Norwegian King to be delivered by Scott if they

failed to make it back to Framheim safely. Planting the Norwegian flag, Amundsen reflected on his momentous achievement: 'The area around the North Pole – devil take it – had fascinated me since childhood, and now here I was at the South Pole. Could anything be more crazy?'

In December the sun never sets in the Antarctic but Amundsen decided to travel at night-time to keep the sunlight on their backs, which reduced the threat of snow blindness when goggles were removed. The Norwegians, all expert skiers, made rapid progress returning north, helped by the 150 snow cairns they had built between supply depots. Each was built

from blocks, cut out of the snow with large snow knives, and inside each one a note was left giving its precise position and directions to the next.

At each camp the men ate their caches of frozen meat and Norwegian pemmican, which differed to the British version in that it was mixed with oatmeal and dried vegetables, more akin to the traditional Inuit recipe, and containing essential carbohydrates and Vitamin C. Amundsen's biscuits contained wholemeal flour, oats and yeast, which also provided Vitamin B.

During his time in the Northwest Passage, Amundsen had learned from the native Netsilik people that caffeine was best avoided while sledging, supplying only cocoa for his men. Experience from the Arctic also taught Amundsen to solder shut his fuel canisters, preventing the kind of leakage that badly affected the British expedition. However, perhaps the greatest lesson Amundsen learned was from the native Inuits of northern Canada with regards to clothing: that furs should be worn loosely when working hard to allow dry air to circulate, but pulled closer to the skin with drawstrings when at rest. This prevented clothes becoming sodden with sweat and losing their insulating properties. Similarly, the integrated hood found on traditional Inuit clothing kept out drafts but allowed warm moist air to be expelled.

Amundsen's sledging mittens were also based on Inuit design, with the fur facing inside to keep hands warm, and a leather outer layer able to grip the harness reins and dog whip. They also provided some protection from the bad-tempered sledge dogs, which were always hungry. On the journey back Amundsen recalled: 'By this time the dogs had already begun to be very voracious. Everything that came in their way disappeared; whips, ski-bindings, lashings, poles etc., were regarded as delicacies. If one put down anything for a moment, it vanished.'

With only eleven sledge dogs harnessed to the two remaining sledges, Amundsen began to pick up the pace. After just ninety-nine days, ten fewer than anticipated, he and his team triumphantly returned to Framheim on the morning of 26 January 1912. Amundsen's first words to the startled camp cook were: 'Good morning, my dear Lindstrøm. Have you any coffee for us?'

Amundsen's men wasted no time packing up the *Fram*, and within four days were sailing back to Tasmania where they announced their success to the waiting press. Congratulations poured in from around the world, although, back in Britain, the news was greeted with mixed emotions. While some felt that Amundsen's change of plans, to head south rather than north, were somewhat underhand; others, such as Ernest Shackleton, applauded his achievements, hailing Amundsen as: 'Perhaps the greatest polar explorer of today'.

In 1956, in a fitting tribute to the courageous men that took part in both the Norwegian and British expeditions, the US scientific research base in Antarctica was named the Amundsen-Scott South Pole Station.

Above left Final observations being made at the South Pole with a sextant and artificial horizon on 17 December 1911.

Above right Photograph by Olav Bjaaland of Roald Amundsen, Helmer Hanssen, Sverre Hassel and Oscar Wisting in front of the tent erected at the South Pole, 16 December 1911.

Lieutenant Colonel Percy Fawcett

Born: 18 August 1867, UK
Disappeared: May 1925, Brazil

Standing at well over six-foot tall in his trademark fedora, with a steely blue gaze and a magnificent Edwardian moustache, Lieutenant Colonel Percy Fawcett was an imposing figure. He won the Royal Geographical Society's prestigious Gold Medal for explorations in South America. However, he also developed a fatal obsession with this hostile environment. Infatuated by the idea that a forgotten city, 'Z', lay hidden in the jungle, in May 1925, he trekked into the wilds of the Amazon basin on his final quest to locate the city and was never seen again.

The Lost City of 'Z' Unpacked

Expedition:
Lost city of 'Z',
Mato Grosso, Brazil

Date:
1925

Length:
Unknown

1. Theodolite
2. Altoids tin for matches
3. Tweed jacket
4. Fedora
5. Waxed tarpaulin
6. Plus fours
7. Sextant
8. Cut-throat razor
9. Sixty gold sovereigns
10. Tobacco pouch
11. Pipe
12. Tinned food
13. Mules
14. Chronometer
15. Signet ring
16. Flares
17. Rifle
18. Mosquito net
19. Powdered milk
20. Accordion
21. Trunks

Having joined the Royal Artillery in 1886, Percy Fawcett served in Malta, Hong Kong and Ceylon (now Sri Lanka) before deciding to retrain as a surveyor with the Royal Geographical Society (RGS). With a growing reputation as a dogged adventurer, he first encountered the Amazon in 1906, when he was sent by the RGS into an uncharted region to help settle a border dispute between Brazil and Bolivia, and fill in, as he put it: 'the last great blank space in the world'. It took Major Fawcett's team eighteen months to map their allotted section, one year ahead of schedule; it was clear that he had found his calling.

Between 1907 and 1914, Fawcett would return to survey the Amazon basin a further five times. All the while his reputation as Britain's foremost explorer grew to celebrity status as fantastic tales of giant venomous spiders, wild double-nosed dogs and flesh-eating parasites grabbed the newspaper headlines. His field notes, which included vivid descriptions of vast unexplored jungle plateaus, were even thought to have inspired Sir Arthur Conan Doyle to write his 1912 adventure novel *The Lost World*.

Amongst these fantastic tales, were of course hazards all too real. The deadliest of all being the mosquito, spreading malaria and dengue fever. Fawcett was well aware of the danger wrought by this tiny insect and always brought mosquito netting along on his expeditions. It kept the mosquitoes at bay but couldn't deter the jungle's vampire bats that would feast on any exposed piece of skin that touched the mesh. In Fawcett's diary he recounts how: 'We awoke to find our hammocks saturated with blood.'

Snakes were also a constant threat, and another diary entry tells the tale of one team member being ambushed by a 7ft (2.75m) bushmaster (a rare but highly venomous snake), striking him in the chest at close range. Leaping into the air he managed to draw his Webley revolver and put two rounds into the head of the creature, before collapsing in a heap fearing the worst. Thankfully, on closer examination he realised that the viper had actually sunk its fangs into his tobacco pouch; soaked in venom it seemed that, this time at least, smoking had saved his life.

It wasn't just the wildlife that posed a threat; Amazonian tribes-people had become mistrustful of Europeans due to plantation owners' notorious reputations for slave raids. However, Fawcett was a skilled and diplomatic explorer who refused to engage aggressively with the local tribes, often striding forth to meet them face-to-face with a cool indifference to the barrage of poison-tipped arrows whizzing back the other way. In one incident, Fawcett's company of canoes had been paddling upstream when they rounded a bend and surprised an encampment on a wide sandbar. Fawcett described in his diary how: 'dogs barked, men shouted, women screamed and reached for their children' as the tribesmen rained down arrows on his company cowering in their boats. Unable to move and short of options, the ever resourceful Fawcett ordered one of his men to play the accordion as loudly as possible to try and defuse the situation. It worked, the bemused natives stopped firing, and a few minutes later Fawcett was greeting the tribespeople and exchanging gifts of friendship.

Despite the dangers, hostilities and mounting financial pressures, it was the First World War that put a hold on his Amazonian expeditions. Fifty years old at the outbreak of war, he felt it was his patriotic duty to volunteer to re-join his old army regiment, and was promptly dispatched to Belgium to command a brigade of gunners in Flanders. By the time hostilities ended Fawcett had been mentioned in dispatches to Field Marshal Haig at least three times, was promoted to Lieutenant Colonel and awarded the Distinguished Service Order.

It was during these war years that Fawcett became increasingly obsessed with the idea that

the Brazilian Amazon still held secrets. On his first expedition in 1906 he had found fragments of intricately designed pottery scattered on the forest floor, which seemed to support the local legends that this area had once been home to advanced civilizations. The Muisca tribe in particular had long told stories of a chief covered in powdered gold and of cities in the rainforests supporting thousands of people and filled with untold riches.

These stories were not new amongst Western explorers, in the mid-16th Century, Spanish conquistadors had already mounted large expeditions into Ecuador and northern Brazil to search for, what they called, El Dorado (The Golden One). In 1595 Sir Walter Raleigh also heard the rumours of a hidden 'city of gold' and took a break from the Spanish-Anglo War, heading 650km (400 miles) inland, up the Orinoco River, to try and claim it for England. But it remained elusive, and by the early 19th Century most people had dismissed the lost city of El Dorado as nothing more than a legend.

Nevertheless, Fawcett's belief that there was a lost city in the Amazon – which he preferred to

call simply, Z 'for the sake of convenience' – was absolutely unshakeable. His conviction that there was a hidden civilization, a jungle equivalent of Atlantis, waiting to be rediscovered, was reinforced by rumours that a race of white-skinned and blue-eyed people had been spotted in that region, and an ornately carved 6-in (15-cm) basalt idol, supposedly discovered in this area, was seen by Fawcett as further proof of advanced ancient cultures. However, by far the most convincing piece of evidence was Manuscript No. 512, discovered by Fawcett in the archives of the Rio de Janeiro National Library in 1920. This tatty worm-eaten document, from an ill-fated Portuguese mining expedition in 1743, mentions the same fair-skinned men living close to a vast ruined city atop a range of mountains to the north of Mato Grosso. In great detail the report describes a large stone-built settlement, damaged by earthquakes but with paved roads, grand statues atop carved columns, sealed vaults inscribed with strange symbols and hidden among the rubble a bow, carved figurines and large gold coins.

Impatient and fixated, Fawcett launched himself into a hastily prepared expedition in 1920, selling half his military pension to fund the journey to Brazil. Poorly equipped and weakened by fever he was eventually forced to turn back after his horse broke its leg and had to be shot. The old soldier wasn't done yet and Fawcett was soon making plans for an eighth foray into the Amazon basin to find the lost city of Z. However, this time, he wasn't the only one.

Competition came in the form of an American multi-millionaire amateur explorer, Dr. Alexander Hamilton Rice, who had assisted Hiram Bingham's expedition that discovered Macchu Picchu in 1911. Rice was now amassing a vast array of expensive equipment and a one hundred-strong team of porters, advisors and cameramen to record and document his quest to find the lost city. Before the First World War, the RGS had watched as one of its most prestigious members, Robert Falcon Scott, was beaten to the South Pole by his Norwegian rival. Now they were in a quandary: sceptical that any large civilisation could have ever existed in this brutal environment, they were equally determined that no rival should discover the fabled lost city ahead of Britain's most admired explorer.

In the end the RGS supported Fawcett's expedition and supplied some 'exceptionally light survey instruments … including a four-inch theodolite, a three-inch sextant, aneroids (altimeters and barometers that recorded air pressure), compasses and … two half-chronometers engraved R.G.S. Nos. 16 and 24.' Additional items, including a pocket book, goggles and a hypsometer (a device that calculates height above sea level using the boiling point of water), were supplied by scientific instrument makers J.H. Steward, Ltd. of London. With further assistance in the form of a generous gift from the Rockefeller family, some lucrative deals with a consortium of American newspapers and a donation from a mysterious group of London financiers known as The Glove, Fawcett was finally able to fund his eighth and final expedition.

Opposite A young Major Fawcett mapping the frontier between Brazil and Bolivia using a theodolite and tripod.

Bounding off the *Vauban*'s gangplank at Rio de Janeiro in January 1925, Fawcett's well-toned physique belied his fifty-seven years. His companions for the expedition were his eldest son Jack and Jack's closest friend, Raleigh Rimmell. Aged twenty-one and twenty-three the two men were absolute novices when it came to jungle exploration. However, Fawcett preferred to travel in small groups to avoid delays, or being mistaken for a slave trader's raiding party, and believed that Jack and Raleigh's loyalty would see them through.

On the quayside, metal trunks loaded with dried provisions, canned food and powdered milk were unloaded along with survey equipment and other essentials including flares, Winchester rifles, aluminium map tubes and custom-made 18in (45cm) machetes. Fawcett's planning this time was meticulous, whittling his kit list down to the absolute minimum based on years of experience.

On 20 April 1925, Fawcett and the two young men set off from the state capital of Mato Grosso, Cuiabá, on their year-long quest accompanied by two Brazilian porters, two horses, eight mules and a pair of hunting dogs that they christened Pastor and Chulim. They wore lightweight clothing made from a special tear-proof gabardine (a fabric patented by Burberry which could be waterproofed with lanolin), long riding boots and matching fedoras.

On 29 May 1925, Fawcett dispatched – via a local runner – an update to his newspapers and an optimistic letter to his wife to say that they were now at Dead Horse Camp (the spot where he'd put down his lame horse on a previous expedition), signing off: 'You need have no fear of any failure.'

It was from here, between the Xingu and Araguaya Rivers, beyond the 'Snoring Mountains' of the Serra do Roncador, that Fawcett hoped to find his elusive city of Z. He sent his two guides and animals back to Cuiabá, jettisoned everything but the bare essential – including most of the surveying equipment – and with his two young companions set forth to penetrate what the *Washington Post* prophetically described as: 'Land Whence None Returned'.

Heading northeast Fawcett estimated that they would reach Z by August, and the Kalapalo tribe have an oral story from those times of three white explorers heading in that direction from Dead Horse Camp. Their story also describes how the 'chief' carried a rucksack, as his two younger companions limped behind, towards an area of forest where violent tribes were known to inhabit.

The Kalapalo tracked the men for four days, watching campfire smoke coil through the forest canopy each evening, but on the fifth day the fires stopped. Any trace of the men simply disappeared.

EXPEDITIONS UNPACKED

Whether they were killed by hostile tribes, ambushed by renegade soldiers, robbed by bandits, or died of disease, starvation or any number of perils held in the jungle, nobody knows. Some theories even suggest that they found El Dorado and lived out their days worshipped as gods.

Fawcett had left clear instructions that should anything happen to them, no search parties were to be sent after them. Ignoring these requests, however, numerous search parties were launched – both privately and by the RGS.

Various pieces of kit resurfaced in the 1930s, including an engraved nameplate from an equipment supplier, a theodolite and a metal trunk, but most believe these had been deliberately left behind or were relics from earlier expeditions.

In 1979, a British cameraman discovered Percy Fawcett's gold signet ring in a shop in the backstreets of Cuiabá. The ring, which perfectly matched the wax imprint held at the RGS, was inscribed with the Fawcett family motto 'Nec Aspera Terrent' (meaning 'difficulties be damned'). It had been a gift from his two sons; Percy's wife, Nina, was adamant that he would never have given it up willingly.

Newspapers around the globe celebrated Fawcett as one of the greatest archaeological explorers of his age. Some academics and geographers were not so kind, dismissing him as a crank with an absurd obsession for an impossible city.

Yet, 80 years later, in the very spot Fawcett believed he would find Z, archaeologists did discover twenty pre-Columbian earthworks, laid out in precise geometric patterns integrating house platforms, moats and huge palisade walls connected by roads, bridges and plazas, with: 'A sense of engineering and mathematics that rivalled anything that was happening in Europe at the time.' Each settlement could have been home to up to five thousand people which suggests that a sprawling conurbation of perhaps sixty thousand people could have once lived in this region.

It may not have been a stone-built metropolis filled with riches, but Fawcett's unshakeable belief in a once-grand civilisation lost to the jungle was finally vindicated.

Below Major Fawcett and his survey team in the Brazilian rainforests close to the Bolivian border in 1906, filling in 'the last great blank space in the world'.

Eva Dickson

Born: 8 March 1905, Sweden
Died: 24 March 1938, Iraq

Eva Dickson lived life to the full. While she is best remembered for her exploits as an automotive adventurer – and for being the first woman to drive across the Sahara – she was also a pioneering female aviator and a skilled horsewoman. Tall and brimming with self-confidence, Dickson mixed with Sweden's cultural elite throughout the 1920s; posing for some of the country's most celebrated painters, sculptors and photographers and working as a fashion designer for Stockholm's most prestigious couture manufacturer, Märthaskolan. Life was never dull when Dickson was around.

Crossing the Sahara Unpacked

Expedition:
First woman to cross the Sahara by car

Date:
1932

Length:
27 days

1. Chevrolet Confederate
2. Hunting rifle
3. Beret
4. Trenchcoat
5. Driving gloves
6. Engine oil
7. Journals
8. Pots and pans
9. Bible
10. Camera Equipment
11. Spare tyre
12. Gasoline
13. Mechanic's overalls
14. Tool bag
15. Maps
16. Mosquito net
17. Water bag
18. Shovel
19. Petroleum jelly
20. Camping bed

Eva Dickson (née Lindström) was 20 when she married the Swedish rally driver Olof 'Olle' Dickson in the autumn of 1925, following a whirlwind romance. For their honeymoon the car-mad couple drove from Stockholm to Marseilles before shipping their vehicle over to Alexandria and exploring the ancient sites of Egypt. After the birth of their first son, they continued to explore Europe by car, motorcycle and aeroplane, often writing and keeping detailed photo journals of their adventures.

Dickson had learnt to drive in a two-litre Ballot sports tourer (a French manufacturer more famous for its Grand Prix race cars) tearing around the dirt roads of Vagnhärad in south-east Sweden. After she married, her husband introduced her to competitive motorsport, and initially they rallied together as pilot and navigator.

In 1927, Dickson competed in her first major women's car race and quickly proved to be a ferociously competitive driver. As most Swedish motor rallies at this time were male-only events, she would register under the pseudonym of Anton Johansson. With her good looks and devil-may-care attitude she quickly became a media celebrity; 'Anton' even appeared in a newspaper advert for Chevrolet's new six-cylinder sedan.

Dickson certainly never shied away from press attention, and in the summer of 1929 drove her sports car around the centre of Stockholm wearing just her swimwear.

She and her husband separated in the early 1930s and Dickson embarked on a number of long-distance road trips to Paris, Rome and eventually into Africa.

In 1932, while on safari in Kenya, she was introduced to the famous big-game hunter Bror Blixen (the former husband of *Out of Africa* author Karen Blixen) and they soon became lovers, bringing Blixen's second marriage to an end.

One evening, while dining at the European Club in Nairobi, a challenge was laid down by a chauvinistic table guest that would put Dickson in the record books as one of the world's greatest motoring adventurers. She recorded the conversation in her memoirs, *An Eva in the Sahara*:

'Women are impossible nowadays! They paint their nails red, bleach their hair, they drink champagne or smoke cigarettes until the fingertips are brown from nicotine. They don't even have children anymore. Look at yourself, Madame, what is good enough for you?'

'I can drive,' replied Eva.

'Drive a car! Every educated person can drive a car, play bridge and go dancing,' exclaimed her dinner guest haughtily.

'But I'll drive all the way from Nairobi to Algiers.'

'I bet you cannot do it!'

'The bet is accepted. The loser invites everyone to champagne,' Eva laughed.

In the Kenyan capital, Dickson bought a black open-top Chevrolet Confederate – America's best-selling model in 1932 – costing around US$550. Nicknamed the Baby Cadillac it was one of the most comfortable cars of its age. Powered by a 60-horsepower, 3.2-litre straight-six it was capable of an impressive 112km/h (70mph), despite weighing in at a hefty 1.3 tonnes. Within a few weeks Dickson was ready for the journey, modifying the Chevrolet by adding wooden slats to the top of the running boards to create two large external storage bins, and signwriting across both sides of the car in big white letters 'Nairobi – Stockholm'.

All machines of this era were pretty high maintenance in comparison to modern vehicles, with oil changes recommended every 1,600km (1,000 miles) and basic mechanical checks and tweaks required every 800km (500 miles). Drums of engine oil, spare parts and general service items (spare tyres, filters, fuses etc.) had to be squirrelled

aboard into every nook and cranny. Most important of all perhaps were the reserve tanks of gasoline which were needed to increase the vehicle's range, given that gas stations throughout central Africa were pretty sparse at this time. Without these extra fuel supplies the Chevy's 42-litre (11 gallon) tank would have been drained in less than 320km (200 miles). Inside the big four-seater Dickson had also packed a vast array of camping gear, road maps, pots and pans, camera equipment, petroleum jelly for waterproofing the car's electrical system and shovels to dig the wheels out of the soft sand. And never far from her grasp, for her own personal protection, was her trusty hunting rifle.

Originally Dickson planned to take on the challenge alone, but on the day of departure, as she was driving to the garage in Nairobi for final checks, she met a young local man, Hassan Ali, who offered to accompany her for the entire trip.

The first part of their journey through western Kenya and Uganda went without any major setbacks, other than the occasional exploding tyre due to the ferocious desert heat. Apart from the odd toilet break and puncture repair the pair drove non-stop for up to twelve-hour stints before making camp wherever they could. Although Dickson slept in the open air on safari-style camping beds with mosquito netting draped over her, by the time they

reached Sudan she was suffering badly from the symptoms of malaria including a high temperature, aching joints, chills and nausea.

When the 'desert couple', as the press were now calling them, reached eastern Chad, Dickson noted in her journals how the journey was getting much tougher. She was frustrated by the constant punctures and added that they were running low on supplies, were constantly hungry and becoming dangerously dehydrated under the relentless African sun. She also described how she had to frighten off a poisonous snake by dropping her Bible on top of it. But it was in northern Chad that they faced their greatest obstacle as a large wooden bridge had collapsed into the river below. The waters were too deep to drive across but the feisty Swedish adventurer wouldn't give up just yet – she'd made a bet and she was going to win it.

Dickson managed to borrow a horse, and with only three boiled eggs to keep her going, rode for two days to the French commander's post in Bongor on the banks of the Longone River. After little persuasion, 900 men were dispatched to where her stricken Chevy was parked up, and within three days the bridge was completely rebuilt. With the car's freshwater bags fully recharged, and surviving on cold fish buns, the pair eventually made it to the port of Algiers, on the Mediterranean coast

twenty-seven days after leaving Nairobi. The wager was won; Dickson became the first woman to cross the Sahara Desert by automobile – and somebody back at the European Club was facing an extremely large bar bill.

It took several more days of hard driving through a wintery northern Europe before Dickson and Ali reached the final finish point in Stockholm late in the afternoon. Despite the poor weather a cheering crowd welcomed them home, along with several reporters and members of Sweden's Royal Automobile Club. Before the photographers could snap the triumphant couple, a large Chevrolet pennant was stuck in the car's radiator grill; the successful adventure was an unmissable opportunity for Chevy to advertise the reliability of its six-cylinder Confederate.

Details of Dickson's record-breaking adventure appeared in Sweden's *Weekly Journal*, a newspaper that she would briefly work for as a foreign correspondent during the Italo-Ethiopian War.

In 1936, Dickson married Bror Blixen, honeymooning at Ernest Hemingway's property in Key West, Florida. But before she would agree to return with her new husband to Kenya she wanted to have one last motoring adventure.

On 3 June 1937 Eva set out on a solo expedition along the famous Silk Road, all the way from Stockholm to Beijing, following in the footsteps of the great Swedish explorer Sven Hedin. For this trip she bought a Ford Model 78 Convertible, powered by an 85-horsepower 'flathead' V8, and loaded up with supplies and provisions for the epic adventure.

After making good progress through Turkey, Iran and into India she found the northern border was completely closed, following Japan's declaration of war on China. Exhausted, painfully thin and low on funds, Dickson hatched a cunning plan to try and recoup some money by betting an English acquaintance of hers in Calcutta that she could get back to London quicker by car than he could by steamship. Racing back through Iraq in March 1938, Dickson misjudged a bend on a poorly surfaced road on the outskirts of Baghdad one evening. Her car flipped over and tumbled down the mountainside, killing her instantly. She was only thirty-three.

She was buried at the Norra Cemetery near Solna in south-east Sweden, not far from the gravel roads of Vagnhärad where, as a high-spirited teenager, she first fell in love with the motorcar. Dickson is remembered not just for her insatiable thirst for life, but also as a pioneer who showed the establishment that high-octane adventures were not solely the preserve of men.

Above left Dickson, wrapped in her insulated mechanic's overalls, poses with the famous Swedish explorer Sven Hedin in front of her Ford Model 78 Convertible in the summer of 1937.

Above right Dickson crosses the Halys river in Turkey during her ill-starred motoring adventure of 1937: retracing the route of the old Silk Road from Stockholm to Beijing.

Clärenore Stinnes

Born: 21 January 1901, Germany
Died: 7 September 1990, Sweden

Born in Germany, in 1901, Clara Eleonore Stinnes, better known as Clärenore, was the daughter of Germany's wealthiest man, the industrial tycoon Hugo Stinnes. She was a passionate petrolhead from a young age, and by thirteen could name every make and model of motorcar that had ever been made. When her father invited his sons to join the family business, but excluded Stinnes because of her gender, she left home, moved to Berlin and became a racing driver. Despite her motorsport glories, Stinnes craved adventure: her greatest ambition was to become the first person to circumnavigate the globe by car.

Circumnavigation of the Globe Unpacked

Expedition:
First circumnavigation of the globe by production car

Date:
1927–1929

Length:
2 years 1 month

1. Support vehicle
2. Adler Standard 6 saloon
3. Shovels
4. Storage cases
5. Spare tyres
6. Lord, Stinnes' Gordon setter
7. Hard-boiled eggs
8. Snow chains
9. Shirt and tie
10. Camera equipment
11. Evening dress
12. Spare wheel cover
13. Boots
14. Sand ladders
15. Dynamite
16. Vodka
17. Jerrycans
18. Grey flannel breeches
19. Tent
20. Hat
21. Mauser pistols
22. Ammunition

Despite Clärenore Stinnes' family's vast wealth, they did not approve of her plan to circumnavigate the globe by car and flatly refused to financially support it.

Undaunted, Stinnes negotiated several lucrative sponsorship deals with the German automotive industry, including Frankfurt-based carmaker Adler, who provided her with a dark green and burgundy Standard 6 saloon.

Plucked straight off the production line, the only modifications the car had were the fully reclining seats that converted to a makeshift bed and the large storage cases and shovels that were lashed to the running boards. Signwritten on the rear spare wheel cover, were the various countries the 'Adler Car – Around The World' expedition would be calling in on during its world tour; a journey that Stinnes believed could be completed in twelve months.

Adler, the manufacturer of Germany's first mass-produced motorcar, saw this as a fantastic opportunity to showcase its model around the world. Tyre manufacturers, petroleum companies and makers of electrical car components also joined the public relations spree. As did the arms manufacturer Mauser, who supplied the expedition with three pistols and several boxes of ammunition for personal protection.

Once Stinnes had secured 100,000 Reichsmark, she booked her steamship passages, planning a route through twenty-three countries, with stops at major towns and cities to refuel and resupply. The rest of her costs she hoped to recover by filming her adventures. In the 1920s, travel documentaries were very popular in German cinemas.

It's likely that inspiration for Stinnes' grand expedition came from newspaper stories and newsreels about the American adventurer Aloha Wanderwell, who at just sixteen years old, had answered Walter 'Cap' Wanderwell's advert for a secretary, translator and driver to join him on his race around the world using Indian motorcycles and highly modified Model T Fords. Travelling largely around the northern hemisphere, the Wanderwells took four and half years to travel eastwards from France and in January 1925, Aloha became the first female to girdle the world by automobile.

However, this time, Stinnes was going to be the principal driver, piloting a standard production vehicle. 'Oh God, I want to get to know the world from my own perspective, that's all,' Stinnes told the Austrian reporter, who was curious why this privileged young woman would embark on such a hazardous venture. Smartly dressed in grey

Above The two-tonne Adler Standard 6 is hauled up a boulder track, high in the Peruvian Andes, by a team of hired men and farm animals – July 1928.

flannel breeches, shirt and tie, Stinnes departed Frankfurt on 25 May 1927, accompanied by Carl-Axel Söderström, a Swedish cinematographer she had met only two days earlier, her black Gordon setter, Lord, and two Adler factory mechanics aboard a company truck. Fully laden, this support vehicle carried jerry cans of fuel, tools, food supplies, cooking utensils and a tent, in addition to Söderström's tripod, camera equipment and canisters of film.

With a top speed of just 85km/h (53mph), progress in the overloaded Standard 6 seemed painfully slow to the former racing driver who was more used to high-powered sports cars. Delays due to breakdowns – a clutch change in Prague, axle shafts in the Balkans – soon scuppered Stinnes' meticulous planning, as she averaged just 100km (62 miles) per day.

In Asia the roads deteriorated rapidly, almost toppling the support truck into a ravine on a

narrow mountain pass near Ankara. On the road to Baghdad their thermometer saw daytime temperatures soar to 54°C (130°F) in the shade. The little water they had managed to source 'tastes of mutton fat and old herrings', Stinnes noted in her diary.

After numerous delays and breakdowns the team finally arrived in the Russian capital, well behind schedule, at the beginning of winter. While her advisors in Moscow strongly suggested that they wait until the spring before pushing through Siberia, Stinnes was stubborn and impatient, and couldn't be dissuaded.

Stocking up with three rifles, three evening dresses and 128 hard-boiled eggs for sustenance, they set out east towards the Ural Mountains. After 9,650km (6,000 miles) on the road, the two vehicles finally reached the River Sura.

Running high with winter floodwater, and with only a rickety wooden ferry to cross it, the team had to chop down trees to strengthen the ferryboat's deck before gingerly loading their vehicles aboard. Shortly after this, following days of digging the truck wheels out of deep cloying mud, the two mechanics deserted the expedition, leaving Söderström and Stinnes to battle onwards unsupported. While the Swede admitted in his journal that he wished he'd: 'never embarked on this damn journey', he loyally stood by his new German friend. Braving hungry wolves and breadknife-wielding Russian drunks, the two vehicles continued to limp eastwards along rutted ox tracks.

Using snow chains attached to rear driven wheels the pair ploughed through drifting snow into Siberia. At Kultuk on the southern shores of Lake Baikal, the couple spent ten weeks hunting and filming as they waited for the lake to fully freeze over; as temperatures dropped as low as -53°C (-63°F), the frozen surface of Lake Baikal,

the sixth-largest lake on the planet, offered a tempting short cut to Werchneudinsk 600km (370 miles) to the northeast. With the car weighing close to two tonnes, and the truck considerably more, the two drivers edged gingerly onto the ice road that hugged the lake's fringes. Not long into the journey they watched in horror as a horse and cart crashed through the ice road in front of them and cracks appeared in the surface around them. Flooring the throttle they sped along the frozen lake, making landfall several hours later, and settling their jangled nerves with cheap Russian vodka.

Swapping the painful cold for blistering heat, new perils awaited the couple in the Gobi Desert, between China and Mongolia. After surviving the ferocious heat, blinding sandstorms and avoiding the attentions of feuding Chinese warlords, they were pursued across the desert by armed Hunghuzi bandits on horseback. As they accelerated to make their getaway the carburettor on the support truck,

Below Shovels at the ready. The Adler gets bogged down in watering hole on the road from Peru to Bolivia – November 1928.

carrying all the spare fuel and the highly flammable nitrate film, caught fire.

Stinnes and Söderström had barely put out the flames and got going again, when a leaf spring on the car snapped in two. A few warning shots from their Mausers bought them some time to make hasty repairs, but in the panic one of their sand ladders (metal tracks that provided extra traction in soft sand) got left behind – a costly mistake that led to a lot of laborious shovelling and lost time before they rejoined the surfaced roads of eastern China.

A year after leaving Frankfurt, they now had 30,000km (18,500 miles) behind them and were crossing the Pacific Ocean by steamship towards Hawaii. Rather than taking the easy route across the US mainland, Stinnes was determined to explore South America landing in Peru and heading east across the Andes.

With no useable roads, Stinnes had to hire armies of farm workers, horses and oxen to manhandle the vehicles up the slopes. Where rocks blocked their path, they used dynamite to blast a way through. Where the land was too steep the pair had to improvise with ropes and pulleys to pull the vehicles onwards – sometimes managing just 150m (500ft) in a day.

Exhausted by this foray into South America, they returned to California and began crossing the USA the easy way, where they were welcomed as heroes wherever they went. In Detroit they were greeted by Henry Ford and given a VIP tour of the Ford car plant. They even received an invite to the White House from President Hoover.

Their twenty-five-month journey, which had taken them through twenty-three countries, ended on 24 June 1929 with their arrival in Berlin. With two huge garlands tied to the vehicles' radiators, the triumphant adventurers paraded around the famous Avus circuit, where Stinnes had taken so many of her motor-racing victories – under the

EXPEDITIONS UNPACKED

pseudonym Miss Lehmann – just a few years earlier. Through ice and heat, bogs and boulders, the couple had forged new roads through distant lands where there were no maps, petrol stations or mechanics' workshops. As they turned off their engines for the very last time, the Standard 6's odometer showed a total trip distance of 46,298km (28,768 miles).

Although Söderström was already married, privately, the two globetrotters had become very close. He divorced soon after his return to Europe, and on 20 December 1930, he and Stinnes were married. Back at the family home in Sweden, hours of movie footage from the expedition were edited to produce one of Germany's earliest road movies entitled *Across Two Worlds by Car*.

Over the next five decades the couple tended their farm, raised three children and fostered several more, until, in November 1976, at eighty-two years old, Söderström passed away.

Stinnes herself lived until the ripe old age of eighty-nine, and continued to enjoy driving, regularly making the long commute between Sweden and Germany. In a rare interview given just before her death she admitted to feeling a little aggrieved that her achievements had been largely forgotten, partly, she felt, because she was a woman.

While Guinness World Records recognises Aloha as the first female to drive around the world, they credit Stinnes with the first circumnavigation by car.

In 2009, a German film crew set out to create a fitting legacy for this tenacious automotive adventurer. Using Söderström's detailed journals, over 1,400 photographs and hours of film footage as source material, the feature-length docudrama *Miss Stinnes Travels the World* was released, to tell the amazing true story of Stinnes, the first person in history to circumnavigate the globe at the wheel of a standard production vehicle.

Amelia Earhart

Born: 24 July 1897, USA

Disappeared: 2 July 1937, central Pacific Ocean

The granddaughter of a wealthy Federal Judge, Amelia Earhart was brought up in the affluent neighbourhood of Atchison, Kansas, but much preferred the rough and tumble of outdoor life. According to legend, her interest in aviation began at six years old when she lashed together a homemade ramp on top of the family's toolshed, inspired by a ride she had seen at the 1904 St. Louis World Fair. Picking herself up, with a fat lip and ripped dress, from the remains of the wooden crate she'd just ridden down the makeshift rollercoaster, she exclaimed to her sister: 'Oh, Pidge, it's just like flying!'

Flight Across the Atlantic Unpacked

Expedition:
First woman to fly solo across the Atlantic Ocean

Date:
1932

Length:
15 hours

1. Western Electric Model 13C radio transmitter
2. Emergency life raft
3. Flight suit
4. 600-horsepower Pratt & Whitney radial engines
5. Rouge
6. Cat's Paw heel
7. Flight cap
8. Handheld Mk 3 aircraft octant
9. Jacket zipper
10. St. Joseph's liniment
11. Parachutes
12. Dr. C.H. Berry's Freckle Ointment
13. Campana Italian Balm
14. Compact mirror
15. Bendix radio direction finder
16. Shoes
17. Sperry GyroPilot
18. Shirt and tie (beneath flight suit)
19. Flight goggles
20. Sextant
21. Leather flying jacket
22. Bone-handled pocketknife
23. Model 20B receiver
24. Lockheed Electra 10E

In December 1920, aged twenty-three, Amelia Earhart took her first real flight – a $10, ten-minute joyride from an airfield in Long Beach, California. 'By the time I had got two or three hundred feet off the ground,' she said, 'I knew I had to fly.'

For the next few years she scrimped and saved, working as a filing clerk at the Los Angeles Telephone Company, to raise the US$1,000 needed to begin her flying lessons. Fully committed to becoming a qualified pilot, she cropped her hair short and bought a leather flying jacket, which she slept in for several nights to give it an appropriately distressed look.

By the middle of 1921, Earhart had scraped enough money together to buy her first aircraft, a bright-yellow Kinner Airster biplane. At the beginning, the trainee pilot was not the best flyer, stalling *The Canary,* as the Airster became known, soon after take off as she climbed to clear a group of trees. Nevertheless, the crash was soon forgotten and Earhart's confidence began to soar. Twenty-one months after her first flying lesson, Earhart set a new altitude record for female pilots, reaching a height of 4,267m (14,000ft), and shortly after, became the sixteenth woman in the USA to be awarded a pilot's licence.

In June 1928, Earhart shot to fame when she was invited to join the pilots Wilmer Stultz and Louis Gordon aboard their Fokker Trimotor to become the first woman to fly across the Atlantic. Since most of the flight was done by instruments, and Earhart was unfamiliar with the large triple-engined monoplane, she did not pilot the aircraft herself and was tasked with keeping the flight log.

After landing in Burry Port, Wales, she modestly admitted to the waiting press that: 'Stultz did all the flying – had to. I was just baggage, like a sack of potatoes … maybe someday I'll try it alone.'

With her newfound celebrity status, Earhart promoted her own line of travel luggage and 'active living' clothing through department stores such as Macy's. Beech-Nut chewing gum and Lucky Strike cigarettes also offered lucrative sponsorship deals that would help finance her future flying adventures.

In August 1928, piloting a British-built Avro Avian biplane that she had brought back from the UK, Earhart became the first female to fly solo across the US mainland and back again.

In May 1932, at the controls of a long-range Lockheed Vega monoplane, Earhart became the first female aviator to cross the Atlantic, and three years later, the first pilot to fly solo 3,860km (2,400 miles) across the Pacific from Hawaii to California. Although America's most famous aviator had now set seven speed and endurance world records, the prize she most hungered for was: 'a circumnavigation of the globe as near its waistline as could be.'

Right Earhart pictured in front of her modified Lockheed Electra 10E. Almost all the windows in the fuselage had been covered to accommodate the long-range fuel tanks.

With a $50,000 grant from Purdue University, Earhart's Lockheed Electra 10E, powered by two 600-horsepower Pratt & Whitney radial engines, was custom-built at the Burbank factory, where major modifications were made to the fuselage and wings to accommodate long-range fuel tanks. Although other pilots had flown around the globe before, Earhart's intended flight plan, following a roughly equatorial route, would be the longest at 46,670km (29,000 miles). Carrying 4,357 litres (1,151 gallons) of aviation fuel, the modified Electra could cruise at 305km/h (190mph) for more than twenty hours of flight time.

Earhart took delivery of her aircraft, registration number NR16020, on her thirty-ninth birthday. Officially named the *Flying Laboratory*, it was a test bed for a variety of new avionics, and was equipped with state-of-the-art communication equipment, including the latest Western Electric Model 13C radio transmitter, Model 20B receiver, and a Beat Frequency Oscillator for sending Morse code messages.

Earhart and her navigator, Fred Noonan, left Miami, Florida, on 1 June 1937. They headed eastwards to take advantage of favourable wind patterns. After hopping along the northeast coast of South America, Earhart left Natal, Brazil, on 7 June 1937 for the 3,198 km (1,727 nautical mile) transatlantic flight to Saint-Louis, Senegal.

Although visibility was bad, and Earhart complained that her wireless worked poorly, Noonan was a skilled celestial navigator. Using his handheld Mk 3 aircraft octant he was able to guide Earhart to the airstrip in Saint-Louis to complete the flight in a record-breaking 13 hours 22 minutes.

On 15 June 1937, Earhart made the world's first non-stop crossing of the Red Sea from Eritrea to India. On these long flights, over featureless expanses of water, Earhart made use of the gyropilot mounted on top of the Electra's instrument panel. This automatic pilot system received information from several other instruments, and its small internal gyroscope, to maintain the aircraft's compass heading and altitude.

After delays in Indonesia, due to monsoon rains and an unfortunate bout of dysentery, Earhart and Noonan finally landed in Darwin, Australia, on 29 June 1937 to make final preparations

for the longest and most perilous part of the circumnavigation: the 4,124km (2,227 nautical mile) flight from Lae, Papua New Guinea, to Howland Island in the central Pacific, where an airstrip had been specially constructed and two naval officers waited with fuel, water, food and spare parts for the penultimate leg to Honolulu.

On the airfield in Lae the engines were serviced, fuel tanks were brimmed and every scrap of surplus equipment, including the parachutes, were stripped from the aircraft to reduce weight and increase its range.

Photographs were taken which show the couple looking relaxed – Earhart in her short-sleeved plaid shirt speaking to sponsors and well-wishers, or posing for the press at the controls of her Lockheed wearing her trademark leather flying jacket.

After final checks Noonan estimated that they had fuel for less than 4,630km (2,500 nautical miles). There was little room for error. Using every inch of the 915m (3,000ft) dirt airstrip, the overloaded Electra dropped off the end of the clifftop runway, then climbed northeastwards into grey overcast skies.

To help locate Howland Island – a remote 4.5 sq km (1,100 acre) speck in the vastness of the Pacific Ocean – the U.S. Coast Guard cutter *Itasca* was stationed off its shores. In the early hours of 2 July 1937, it began to receive radio contact from the Earhart aircraft.

At 6.15 a.m. Earhart reported that they were 320km (200 miles) away. At 6.45 a.m., 160km (100 miles) from the landing strip, she asked the Coast Guard to take a bearing off her radio signals, but the frequency she was using was too high for the *Itasca*'s direction finder.

In a desperate attempt to signal their position, the *Itasca* belched out a 16km (10 mile) trail of dense black smoke. Yet, an hour later, Earhart's frantic voice burst over the ship's loudspeaker: 'We must be on you but cannot see you … gas is running low. Have been unable to reach you by radio … .'

She then asked *Itasca* to send out a radio signal so she could use the Electra's radio direction finder. By turning the loop aerial, located above the cockpit and linked to a degree indicator, they should have been able to take a bearing on

the cutter's signal. However, neither Noonan or Earhart were skilled radio operators; the 75m (250ft) trailing antenna that would have doubled the range of their voice transmissions had been left behind in Miami and neither aviator was proficient with Morse code.

At 8.43 a.m., as the Lockheed's fuel tanks ran dry, the *Itasca* received a final plaintive transmission from Earhart: 'We are on the line 157 337. We will repeat this message. We will repeat this on 6,210 kilocycles. Wait.' Then nothing. All further attempts to contact the Electra were fruitless.

Over the next few weeks the largest rescue mission in history was launched, involving 3,000 men, ten ships and one hundred and two aircraft. The hope was that if they had ditched the plane the empty fuel tanks would have allowed the Electra to float for long enough to launch the emergency life raft, which was automatically inflated by CO_2 cylinders.

Over the last eighty years numerous theories about the fate of Amelia Earhart and her navigator Fred Noonan have been proposed.

Three years after their disappearance evidence emerged that the pair might have come down near an uninhabited coral atoll called Gardner Island (now Nikumaroro), 644km (400 miles) southeast of Howland Island. A series of correspondences between the island's British officials describe how a partial human skeleton, badly damaged by coconut crabs, was found under a ren tree close to an old campfire. While they were originally dismissed as the ancient bones of a shipwrecked native man, modern forensic techniques, comparing photographs with the recorded dimensions of the skeleton, suggest they were a good match for the tall and slender Amelia Earhart. However, the bones were mislaid years ago, and no DNA evidence exists.

Close to the human remains the 1940 report describes finding the charred bones of fish, birds and turtles, as well as a Brandis & Sons sextant box with an inverting eyepiece often used by aviators.

A distinctive Benedictine liqueur bottle – a tipple that Earhart was known to be fond of – was also reported to have been found nearby.

For decades The International Group for Historic Aircraft Recovery (TIGHAR) have been searching the ren tree site for further clues, and in 2001 unearthed a broken bone-handled pocketknife, of the same brand known to be carried by Earhart, and a brass zipper pull from the mid 1930s stamped 'Made in USA'. Other artefacts have included fragments of plexiglas that matched the curvature of the Electra's windows and a Cat's Paw heel dating from the time of Earhart's disappearance, similar to ones she is seen wearing in press photos.

On further investigations at the site in 2012, TIGHAR discovered what they believe to be the contents of Earhart's beauty case. Fragments of a small jar are thought to have contained Dr. C.H. Berry's Freckle Ointment. Another green bottle had possibly contained St. Joseph's Liniment, which was often used for joint pain and as a mosquito repellant. This broken bottle was partially melted and may have been used by a survivor to boil drinking water. Chemical analysis of another small bottle revealed it had contained Campana Italian Balm, an American hand lotion popular in the 1930s, while a fourth shattered bottle, with 'Mennen' embossed in Art Deco lettering, held traces of cosmetic rouge. Close by were two shards of beveled glass from a compact mirror – press photos show Earhart using something similar at the airfield in Darwin.

While TIGHAR's evidence is compelling, it is not definitive proof, and no verifiable wreckage from the Electra has ever been recovered.

Whatever her fate, it is more important that we focus on what this remarkable woman achieved in her short lifetime rather than the mysteries that surround her disappearance.

While this final grand adventure claimed her life, Earhart's legacy, as one of history's greatest aviators, lives on to this day.

Thor Heyerdahl

Born: 6 October 1914, Norway
Died: 18 April 2002, Italy

Eminent ethnologist Thor Heyerdahl first heard the local legends of a king who had led his people to Polynesia from a distant land when he was sat around a campfire on the island of Fatu Hiva in French Polynesia in 1937. Over the next decade Heyerdahl began to uncover surprising connections between South American and Polynesian archaeology and eventually the story of the Peruvian high priest *Kon-Tiki*, whose people were defeated in battle and fled westwards across the Pacific. Intrigued by whether indigenous South Americans could really have sailed 8,000km (4,300 nautical miles) on crude, balsa wood rafts, he decided there was only one way to find out.

Kon-Tiki Expedition Unpacked

Expedition:
Peru to Polynesia by authentic Inca raft

Date:
1947

Length:
101 days

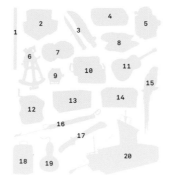

1. Sealed bamboo rods
2. Eight cardboard boxes
3. Morakniv metal knives
4. Shark Powder
5. Bolex 16mm movie camera
6. Sextant
7. Coconuts
8. Sweet potato
9. Watch
10. Robot 35mm camera
11. Guitar
12. Gibson Girl survival radio
13. National NC-173 radio receiver
14. Medical chest
15. Parrot
16. Eight-foot hand harpoons
17. Short razor-sharp machete
18. Paraffin lamp
19. Bottle gourd Lagenaria vulgaris
20. Kon-Tiki

EXPEDITIONS UNPACKED

In Thor Heyerdahl's lifetime, the established academic belief was that Polynesia had been settled by travellers from Asia around 5,500 years ago. However, Heyerdahl thought otherwise. He noticed striking similarities between the half-buried statues found on Easter Island and those at Lake Titicaca in Bolivia and was convinced that fleets of Peruvian rafts could have used the Pacific's Humboldt Current and the strong trade winds to carry them westwards.

To test his theory, and attempt one of history's most daring voyages of experimental archaeology, Heyerdahl decided to build a historically correct replica raft and find the right crew to man it on a repeat of that original voyage.

Nine giant balsa trees were felled from the jungles of Ecuador and transported to the Callao naval dockyards in Lima. Building the raft to a design described by the Spanish conquistadors meant that not a single nail or screw would be used; instead, thick hemp ropes tied the balsa logs together, on top of which a deck of split bamboo was laid. A small open cabin was built towards the stern from bamboo canes, with a banana leaf roof, while strong mangrove wood poles formed the raft's mast and steering oar. About a third of the raft's propulsion was to come from ocean currents, the rest from the prevailing trade winds. To keep the raft on course five pine planks were driven between the logs to act as centreboards, similar to those used on rafts during Inca times.

When it came to crew selection Heyerdahl's primary concern was choosing a team that could work together under extreme conditions, rather than sailing experience: 'I did not want to have it argued afterwards, when we had completed the voyage, that we made it because we were better seamen than the old raft-builders in Peru.'

Herman Watzinger, a technical engineer, was the first to join the *Kon-Tiki*'s crew – the raft was named after the Inca sun god. Bengt Danielsson acted as quartermaster and Spanish translator, while Erik Hesselberg became the ship's navigator, using his watch and sextant to plot the raft's progress across the Pacific. Knut Haugland and Torstein Raaby, both decorated Norwegian resistance fighters, were recruited to man the National NC-173 radio receiver. Using the call sign LI2B, the *Kon-Tiki* was able to keep in contact with stations on both sides of the Pacific. As emergency backups a pair of British Mark II Sabotage transmitters and a Gibson Girl hand-cranked survival radio were also stowed on board.

On 28 April 1947 the *Kon-Tiki* hoisted its square mainsail, decorated with a painted image of the sun king, to begin its long voyage west, just as Heyerdahl believed Polynesia's Peruvian ancestors had done 1,500 years earlier. The decks were littered with baskets of fresh fruit and other gifts that had been hurled on board by well-wishers at the last moment; these included a Spanish-speaking parrot called Lorita, who became the seventh member of the crew.

Few of the South American dignitaries and military personnel waving from the quayside thought the rough-and-ready raft had any chance of surviving the one-hundred-day voyage; one troubled onlooker thrust a Bible on to Heyerdahl for luck, while the pessimistic naval attaché bet 'all the whisky the members of the crew could drink for the rest of their lives' if they reached the South Sea islands in one piece.

As well as the raft's construction, the *Kon-Tiki* expedition wanted to test other ancient technologies that would have been employed to survive the voyage. Two hundred coconuts and sweet potatoes were carried on board and freshwater was stored in bottle gourds and sealed bamboo rods. By the second day at sea, just as they had hoped, they sailed through shoals of sardines and were visited by yellowfin tuna, bonitos and other delicious species. Two 16kg (35lb) dorado were soon caught on the baited dragline, which fed the crew for several days, fried on the *Kon-Tiki*'s small primus stove.

As the raft was swept further northwest towards the equator, the ever-present flying fish became the crew's staple food. Attracted by the raft's paraffin lamp (a warning to other shipping) the fish would launch themselves at the raft during the night, striking the sail and bamboo cabin, marooning themselves on the slatted deck ready for the breakfast chef to collect the next morning.

As well as porpoises, whales and the odd sea turtle, the *Kon-Tiki*'s less welcome visitors were the sharks. After a week at sea a 2.5m (8ft) blue shark had to be bullied away with hand harpoons, but 650km (400 miles) south of the Galapagos Islands, Haugland spotted something more worrying off the stern: 'It was the head of a veritable sea monster, so huge and so hideous that, if the Old Man of the Sea himself had come up, he could not have made such an impression on us.'

A 15m (50ft) whale shark, the largest fish known to man, began taking an unhealthy interest in the *Kon-Tiki*. 'Grinning like a toad' its 1.5m (5ft) wide mouth contained 3,000 teeth and could have turned the *Kon-Tiki* to driftwood in an instant. After an hour of menacing circling, the whale shark moved in, dipping just below the raft. Fearing the worst, Hesselberg drove his harpoon into the monster's massive head. The furious wounded whale shark thrashed desperately, turning the sea to

Below Thor Heyerdahl crouches in front of the raft's cooking box containing the small primus stove where the men fried flying fish for breakfast most mornings.

Opposite The *Kon-Tiki*'s deck littered with shark, flying fish and bonitos, caught on lines and 2.5m (8ft) hand harpoons.

Right A view from the crow's nest shows the raft's bamboo and balsa construction as the men eat a meal on deck and drink from metal water flasks.

Opposite top A large square mainsail was hung from a mast fashioned from tough mangrove wood.

Opposite bottom left Erik Hesselberg with his guitar.

Opposite bottom middle Crew members man the *Kon-Tiki*'s National NC-173 radio receiver.

Opposite bottom right Thor Heyerdahl in the raft's bamboo cabin working at his typewriter.

angry foam, just yards away from the makeshift raft, trying to dislodge the steel harpoon from its skull, before finally disappearing into the ocean's depths.

Various governments lent their support to the *Kon-Tiki* expedition in exchange for the crew carrying out various trials. The British had developed a shark repellent – Shark Powder – although seemingly with little success. While the American government asked Heyerdahl's men to 'field test' an array of their latest equipment, including waterproof matches, floating kitchen utensils, splash-proof sleeping bags, ration packs and fifty-six special plastic containers to supplement the water stored using Inca technology.

Inside the cabin were eight cardboard boxes that had been waterproofed with bitumen. Two contained the medical chest, charts, compass, sounding rope and other scientific equipment, while the remainder were allocated to each of the crew. Hesselberg's contained a guitar and his painting supplies. Danielsson's was the heaviest; as

an avid reader he'd brought seventy-three scientific volumes to make the best use of his free time. While to record the expedition there was a 16mm movie camera and Hesselberg had a Robot 35mm (a compact camera that had been standard issue to Luftwaffe pilots in the Second World War).

Two months into their journey, the crew was still in good spirits. While the stored water was starting to taste a little stale there was more rainfall in this part of the ocean to recharge their supplies, and there was still no shortage of fresh fish. Tiny crabs had started to colonise the seaweed that now clung to the *Kon-Tiki* and added a bit of variety to the crew's diet.

However, the balsa wood hull was starting to deteriorate and had become increasingly water-logged, sinking several inches lower in the water than when they'd left Lima. The ropes had also begun to slacken and cut into the wood, but it was difficult to survey the decay under the raft due to loitering sharks.

THOR HEYERDAHL

EXPEDITIONS UNPACKED

Above left Crew members bring equipment ashore as *Kon-Tiki* runs aground on the Raroia atoll in Polynesia.

Above right The Kon-Tiki's mainsail, decorated with the Sun King's bearded face, is repurposed as a makeshift shelter.

Nevertheless, despite the creaking and banging, the loosely lashed raft tended to roll over the waves in a severe storm, rather than crash into the peaks and troughs as a solid vessel would – it seemed that the old Inca design was well-suited to long ocean voyages after all.

What the crew feared most in this part of the Humboldt Current could be seen lurking just below the surface on the darkest nights: the phosphorescent eyes of giant octopus. With arms covered in suckers that left ugly scars on large whales, and could kill good-sized sharks, Peruvian oceanographers warned the crew to be on guard at night, where the lamps on deck might attract them on board. To avoid being dragged from their sleeping bags and into the ocean's depths, every man slept with a short razor-sharp machete within grasp, ready to slice through any rummaging octopus tentacles.

By the middle of July 1947, as the radio batteries and provisions were beginning to run dangerously low, there were clues that dry land was not far away: frigate birds reappeared, a line-caught shark threw up starfish from the shallow ocean floor and, floating on the horizon, a stationary lens-shaped cloud told them that their long ocean voyage was coming to an end.

Puka Puka was the first Polynesian island that came within sight; coils of campfire smoke rose through the palm trees, teasing the men with the smells of a delicious welcome breakfast being prepared by friendly islanders, but the strong ocean current soon swept them past. Although most of the crew longed to walk on soft dry sand again, Danielsson wasn't too bothered – he still had three books left to read.

The next morning a pair of hovering clouds signalled the islands of Fangahina and Angatau. For four days they steered towards Angatau, but a treacherous coral reef made it impossible to land the 14m (45ft) raft, despite the best efforts of the islanders and their canoes to tow the *Kon-Tiki* ashore.

This was day ninety-seven of the *Kon-Tiki*'s journey across the Pacific, exactly the same number of days Heyerdahl had predicted it would take to reach this group of islands, travelling at an average speed of less than 3km/h (1.5 knots).

The *Kon-Tiki* drifted for another four days before striking a reef on the Raroia atoll. Desperately clinging to the huge balsa logs, to avoid being cut to pieces on the sharp coral, the crew were pretty battered by the time the raft had crashed its way into the uninhabited islet. Fringed with coconut palms and teeming with red hermit crabs, it was a little piece of paradise after 101 days at sea. Heyerdahl later wrote that they rustled up a fantastic meal on the salvaged primus stove with just these two key ingredients. 'Purgatory was a bit damp,' said Danielsson, 'but heaven is more or less as I'd imagined it.'

In 1950, a documentary film of the *Kon-Tiki* expedition was released, using black and white footage from their 16mm movie camera and narrated by Heyerdahl himself. It won an Oscar at the 24th Academy Awards; as much for the incredible feat of crossing the Pacific on a soggy ramshackle raft, as for their pioneering documentary filmmaking.

Heyerdahl had proven that it was entirely feasible that indigenous Peruvians, using the available technology of the Inca period, could have sailed balsa rafts 7,000km (4,300 miles) across the Pacific to settle the South Sea islands. But sadly, despite Heyerdahl's achievements, the *Kon-Tiki* experiment did little to sway scientific thinking about Polynesia's anthropology during his lifetime.

However, in 2011, sixty-four years after the voyage, a team of scientists from the University of Oslo, studying the DNA of the descendants from the original South Sea islanders, discovered traces of genetic make-up that could only have come from South America, long before the colonization of the Europeans in the 18th Century. For many ethnologists, this was the scientific proof that would finally validate Heyerdahl's theory. It appeared that the islanders' folktales of Tiki and his followers were not mere myths and legends, but may have been inspired by the incredible journeys of Peru's earliest maritime explorers.

Left Using wooden crates and jerry cans for stools, the crew rustle up a fabulous meal of coconut and red hermit crab on the salvaged stove.

Jacques Cousteau

Born: 11 June 1910, France
Died: 25 June 1997, France

Born in southwest France, Jacques-Yves Cousteau joined the École Navale when he was twenty years old. Sadly, his childhood dream of becoming a naval pilot was cut short when he broke both his arms in a horrific car crash that very nearly cost him his life. As part of his recuperation, Cousteau swam every day in the Mediterranean Sea. When his friend, Phillipe Tailliez, loaned him a pair of goggles, an entirely new underwater world was opened up to the inquisitive French mariner. This was the decisive moment when Cousteau realised that his future was not in the air, but under the sea.

Voyages of the Calypso Unpacked

Expedition:
Voyages of the Calypso

Date:
1950s

Length:
Various

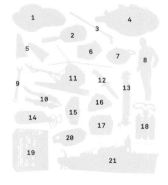

1. SP-500 mini-submarines (nicknamed the Sea Fleas)
2. Depth-pressure-proof camera case
3. Spear-gun
4. SP-350 (nicknamed Denise)
5. Flippers
6. Swimming shorts
7. Open-faced mask
8. Wetsuit
9. Spanner
10. Belt with lead weights
11. Hughes 300C amphibious helicopter
12. Diver's knife
13. Nansen bottle
14. Underwater scooter
15. Rolex Submariner watch
16. Red watch cap
17. Film camera
18. Aqua-Lung
19. Steel shark-proof cage
20. Fernez underwater goggles
21. Calypso

When France fell to the Nazis in 1940, Jacques Cousteau and his family took refuge in the town of Megève, near the Swiss border.

Here, Cousteau continued his passions for filmmaking and underwater exploration. When he wasn't spying on the Italian armed forces and documenting troop movements for the French Resistance, Cousteau and his engineer friend, Émile Gagnan, were hard at work developing an experimental underwater breathing apparatus.

A patent for an open-circuit scuba (self-contained underwater breathing apparatus) system had been filed in 1925. However, it was these two men's adaptation of a gadget that had been designed to run cars on cooking gas that refined the design so that a regulator could deliver the right amount of air to divers as they inhaled. They called it the Aqua-Lung and it is widely hailed as the first practical scuba system.

The first sea trials of their prototype took place in a sheltered cove near Bandol, to avoid being spotted by the occupying Italian troops. Cousteau dived alone watched nervously by his wife, Simone, and the renowned freediver, Frédéric Dumas, who was on hand to rescue him if the bubbles from this Aqua-Lung stopped appearing. As Cousteau later wrote: 'As long as air boiled on the surface all was well below. If the bubbles disappeared there would be anxiety, emergency measures, despair. They roared out of the regulator and kept me company.' The system worked perfectly.

In 1942, Cousteau produced his first film, *Par Dix-huit Mètres de Fond* (*Eighteen Metres Deep*), made off the Île des Embiez in the Mediterranean, using a depth-pressure-proof camera case that

EXPEDITIONS UNPACKED

Cousteau himself had helped to design. For his next film, *Épaves* (*Shipwrecks*), Cousteau could not find the necessary blank movie film, due to the ongoing occupation by the Nazis, and had to buy hundreds of still film reels, intended for a child's toy camera, and glue them together. Despite these technical difficulties, *Épaves* is still considered to be a landmark film in underwater filmmaking.

In both films the scuba equipment used by Cousteau and his team were prototype Aqua-Lung systems, with a mask connected by two hoses to three air cylinders, attached to a backplate and chest harness. In these early warm-water explorations the divers wore little more than open-faced masks, swimming shorts and rubber flippers as they explored the seabed and hunted for fish with their spear-guns.

Before the Cousteau-Gagnan Aqua-Lung was made commercially available in 1946, many French 'hard hat' divers were still wearing the cumbersome copper diving helmets, rubberised suits and lead-weighted boots that had been used since the 1820s. When stronger and more reliable compressed air cylinders became available in the late 1940s, capable of withstanding 200atm, the diving duration of the Aqua-Lung system was extended to more than an hour with the freedom to swim unhindered by ropes and air tubes.

Following the war, Cousteau continued to work with the French Navy clearing underwater mines, while also managing his fledgling scuba business and continuing to develop his submersible camera equipment. Cousteau, along with his old friends Tailliez and Dumas (a trio of divers that became known as the 'musketeers of the sea'), teamed back up in 1948 for the world's first underwater archaeological operation using scuba equipment. Their goal was to film and explore the Roman shipwreck *Mahdia,* a cargo vessel that had sunk off the coast of Tunisia, along with its payload of bronze statues and marble busts. The mission went well, recovering several valuable artefacts.

Although his film of the *Mahdia* expedition, *Carnet de Plongée* (*Dive Logbook*), was well received at the Cannes Film Festival, Cousteau confessed to dinner guests that his dream was to become an oceanographer and obtain an ocean-going vessel to explore the seabed.

British millionaire and former MP Thomas Loel Guinness, who was a great admirer of Cousteau's work, agreed to buy a former Royal Navy minesweeper, the *Calypso*, and lease it to Cousteau for a symbolic one franc a year. Over the next four decades Cousteau was virtually inseparable from his beloved *Calypso,* and during its numerous voyages around the globe, Captain Cousteau was rarely seen away from its bridge without his famous red cap.

However, it was Cousteau's book and subsequent documentary film, *The Silent World* that was to make him a household name. Shot aboard the *Calypso* during its voyages around the Mediterranean Sea, Red Sea, Persian Gulf and Indian Ocean, Cousteau's filmmakers used more than 24km (15 miles) of film in their specialised underwater cameras – only one tenth of which was actually used in the final 1956 release, which was the first feature-length documentary to win an Academy Award.

Watching *The Silent World* it is clear to see that Cousteau was almost as fond of technology as he was of underwater exploration, demonstrating how traditional oceanographic equipment such as the Nansen bottle worked, as well as his high-tech sonar equipment and submersible cameras. Perhaps the most impressive gadgets used by the divers in this film were the underwater scooters. Shaped like a stubby torpedo with handlebars on the back, they were powered by an electric motor which dragged the divers along at impressive speeds, dramatically increasing diving range and duration.

In glorious technicolour, Cousteau filmed blue and grey sharks in the midst of a feeding frenzy,

Opposite Diver wearing an Aqua-Lung swims alongside Jacques Cousteau's two-man 'diving saucer' during an undersea exploration of the Red Sea.

from within a steel shark-proof cage built to his own design. He also discovered the wreck of the *Thistlegorm*, a Second World War cargo ship still fully laden with military motorcycles, armoured personnel carriers and aircraft parts, which has since become one the world's most revered recreational dive sites.

Throughout the 1950s the *Calypso* was steadily upgraded to become a state-of-the-art expedition vessel that also served as a floating film set for Cousteau's diving films. The bulbous bow was fitted with several observation windows that extended 3m (10ft) below the waterline and a diving hatch was fitted in the ship's hull. In 1959, *Calypso* was further modified to accommodate the SP-350, a two-man diving saucer nicknamed *Denise* that could submerge to 350m (1,150ft), manoeuvred by electric-powered water jets that allowed it to travel in all directions. Lying prone on *Denise*'s hull, the two pilots navigated and operated the sampling arm and grab through the small tilted portholes.

In 1975, Cousteau famously used the *Denise* to locate the wreck of the *Britannic*, sister ship to the *Titanic*, sunk off the Greek mainland by an enemy mine in 1916.

In 1965, the SP-350 was joined by two SP-500 mini-submarines, nicknamed the *Sea Fleas*. Roughly 2 x 3m (7 x 10ft) in size and weighing nearly two tons, they looked like a sea turtle with its head and feet pulled in. Piloted by a fighter plane joystick, the 7.5cm (3in) thick Plexiglas portholes allowed Cousteau and his team to dive to 500m (1,640ft), filming by the light of the *Sea Fleas*' powerful search lights. However, Cousteau's favourite gadget joined the ship's crew in the mid-1970s when *Calypso* underwent a major refit for a helipad over the rear decks to accommodate *Felix*, an amphibious helicopter fitted with inflatable pontoons, used for survey work and filmmaking.

Cousteau's personal equipment also improved as technologies evolved. In many of his later films, set in cooler climes, the *Calypso*'s divers famously wore matching black and yellow dive suits, originally made by the American firm EDCO from a revolutionary new neoprene material that had originally been designed as automotive insulation. 'Wetsuits', as they became known, worked by trapping a thin layer of water between skin and the suit, which was quickly warmed by the body's heat, while the small closed air cells of the neoprene offered excellent insulation against further heat

Far left Aboard his prototype shark cage Cousteau is lowered into the water to film these magnificent predators up close.

Left Wearing his cold-water neoprene diving suit, one of *Calypso*'s divers is able to carry out underwater archaeology.

loss. Matching hoods, boots and gloves worked in exactly the same way to keep divers' extremities warm during deeper dives. To counteract this additional buoyancy, Cousteau also wore a belt with lead weights attached, as well as a large diver's knife, which could be jettisoned if he needed to rapidly ascend in an emergency.

One of the most important pieces of equipment used in the early days of scuba diving was the diver's watch. Cousteau formed a close working relationship with several watchmakers who were keen for the *Calypso*'s divers to promote their products and field test their designs in extreme conditions. During the filming of *The Silent World*, Cousteau and his team wore prototype Rolex Submariner watches, which had been designed to withstand water pressure at a depth of 100m (330ft) and remain totally waterproof. Large and robust, with a prominent display, the key design feature was its rotating bezel, which the wearer could zero to the minute hand to calculate the length of the dive more easily. The bezel on a diving watch only turns anticlockwise as a failsafe feature, which would not over extend the dive time if accidentally rotated. Cousteau characteristically wore his Rolex loose, to allow it to be worn over his neoprene gloves.

While some criticised Cousteau's early films for mistreating animals, in later life he was a fervent environmentalist, setting up the Cousteau Society, which attracted almost half a million members. In 1981, he foresaw the growing menace of plastics in the sea; his film *Clipperton: The Island Time Forgot* poignantly ends with a shot of a crab crawling over a doll's head among a mound of plastic that had washed up on the Pacific island's shore. Nevertheless, he was an optimist: 'If we were logical, the future would be bleak, indeed. But we are more than logical. We are human beings, and we have faith, and we have hope, and we can work.'

Aboard the *Calypso*, this celebrated French explorer, inventor, filmmaker and conservationist sailed the globe for almost half a century, educating millions about the ocean's hidden wonders and fighting for their protection. By his death in 1997, he had authored or co-authored more than eighty books, produced 120 TV documentaries and won three Oscars for his ground-breaking feature films.

From that life-changing sea swim with his borrowed goggles, Cousteau's passion for marine exploration never dimmed. As he himself once said: 'The sea, once it casts its spell, holds one in its net of wonder forever.'

Sir Edmund Hillary

Born: 20 July 1919, New Zealand
Died: 11 January 2008, New Zealand

Edmund Hillary grew up on a small family bee farm on New Zealand's North Island. He grew tough helping on the land, collecting and stacking the 40kg (90lb) boxes of honeycomb and suffering up to a hundred bee stings a day. It was at university in the late 1930s that Hillary's love for climbing and the great outdoors grew, before the Second World War stopped play and he joined the Royal New Zealand Air Force as a navigator, serving aboard Catalina flying boats in the South Pacific.

Everest First Ascent Unpacked

Expedition:
First ascent of
Mount Everest

Date:
1953

Length:
11 weeks

1. Goggles
2. Crampons
3. Woollen flat cap
4. Kodak Retina camera
5. Rucksack
6. Custom-made boots
7. Primus camping stove
8. Climbing suit
9. Woollen base layer
10. Walkie-talkies
11. Woollen socks
12. Neck gaiters
13. Heavy cotton dress shirt
14. Mid layers
15. Mid layers
16. Notebook
17. Hat
18. Sleeping bag
19. Open-circuit oxygen regulators
20. Kendal Mint Cake
21. Woollen long john
22. Base layers
23. Sardines, biscuits, tinned apricots
24. Ice axe
25. Woollen pullover
26. Nylon and cotton tent

After the war Edmund Hillary returned to his father's bee keeping business, spending all his free time hiking and climbing. But he wasn't there for long.

In 1951, Hillary was offered a role in a Himalayan reconnaissance expedition, due to his membership of the New Zealand Alpine Club.

Two years later, in March 1953, he was part of the British-led attempt on Mount Everest. This expedition involved more than 400 people, including twenty Sherpa mountain guides and 350 Nepalese porters carrying 4.5 tonnes (10,000lb) of supplies, plus another twelve men to carry the money bags of coins needed to pay them all.

For two months the mountaineers pushed upwards, setting up a series of camps as they forged their way through the Khumbu Icefall towards the Western Cwm.

Trudging above the snow line in spiked steel crampons, around thirty-five members made up the final assault team carrying 20kg (44lb) of state-of-the-art equipment each in their aluminium-framed military-issue rucksacks.

This equipment included specially designed walkie-talkies, which had their plastic components replaced with rubber so they wouldn't shatter in the intense cold. The two-way radios allowed the climbers to stay in touch with base camp almost two miles away, but they weighed in at a hefty 2.27kg (5lb) apiece and had to kept warm by being tucked into underwear.

This expedition saw the pioneering use of synthetic fibres in mountaineering clothing, including Hillary's 'cotton wrap, nylon weft' windproof climbing suit and his wicking base layers. However, much of the team's clothing was still made from traditional natural fabrics such as cotton dress shirts, string vests and custom-made scarves and 'jumperssuits' made from fine Shetland wool.

Low temperatures and strong winds were not the only hazards facing Hillary and the team as they climbed. Snow blindness inflicted excruciating pain, caused by increased exposure to the sun's UV rays as they reflected off the snow and scorched the eye's cornea. The team protected themselves with aviator-style goggles with darkened glass lenses and leather side shields. However, for much of the climb, Hillary's most prized possession was a peaked blue-striped sun hat, hand-sewn by his sister-in-law, with long cotton flaps which also protected his face and neck from the ferocious glare of the sun.

On reaching the South Col, a wind-blasted notch 914m (3,000ft) below the summit, Hillary and his comrades entered a region known as the Death Zone. At this altitude the human body is only able to take in about thirty per cent of the oxygen it normally would at sea level; the blood thickens, heart rates soar and cells start to die. Even the most basic tasks take superhuman amounts of effort and judgement can become seriously impaired without the use of supplemental oxygen. For that reason equipment was selected that was efficient, simple to use and as lightweight as possible.

Particular attention was paid to footwear since it was calculated that, in terms of energy used, every pound removed from the weight of your boots was the equivalent of five pounds removed from your rucksack. Conventional leather arctic boots had thin and poorly insulated uppers and heavy thick soles that made climbing difficult. But with help from the Shoe & Allied Trades Research Association (SATRA), and the shoemakers of Northamptonshire, the Everest high-level assault boot was developed, which had nearly 2.5cm (1in) of felt and kapok insulation beneath a waterproof inner membrane, and a thin microcellular rubber sole designed by Dunlop. Weighing forty per cent less than the traditional Swiss design it was proudly claimed by SATRA that none of the mountaineers who wore them on the 1953 Everest expedition suffered from frostbite on their feet.

Since heading out from Kathmandu various types of tent had been used, but the model favoured

Opposite Edmund Hillary amid the ice pinnacles of the Khumbu Glacier wearing his homemade sun hat and aluminium-framed rucksack.

by the thirty-five team members selected for the final ascent were two-man tents made of the same cotton-nylon fabric as the climbers' outerwear, with waterproof sewn-in groundsheets. At almost 7kg (15lbs) they were quite bulky, but their simple A-shaped poles meant they were easy to erect, even in high winds, and the neat sleeve entrances kept the drifting snow at bay. The thick down-filled sleeping bags had also been cleverly designed with a slippery nylon inner to allow easy movement and could be pulled over the head to conserve body heat, while inflatable rubber mattresses provided extra insulation from the cold ground.

Another problem faced by the Everest team as they set up camp in the Death Zone was that digestive systems tended to shut down just at the point when they most needed the energy stores for that last big push. Further down the mountain, where porters were plentiful, the team had the choice of five types of meat, four types of vegetables, cake, tinned fruit and various other luxuries as part of their general-purpose 'compo' ration box. However, at very high altitude, where the economy of weight was a top priority, a special vacuum-packed 'assault'

ration was developed with around 3,000 calories worth of lemonade powder, sugar, oatmeal, sweets and biscuits, supplemented with a few chosen goodies picked from the 'luxury box'.

But perhaps the most prized treat was Kendal Mint Cake, an incredibly sweet, but easily digestible, high-energy snack bar made from sugar, syrup and peppermint oil. Just one week before the expedition set off for Nepal, one of the team noticed an advertisement for the mint cake in a climbing magazine and swiftly placed an order for 17kg (38lb) of the stuff – roughly the payload of one Nepalese porter. Confectionery was still rationed in Britain after the Second World War, so the shop owner and his staff pooled their ration coupons together to meet the climber's request.

Five days after reaching the South Col, the first assault party of Tom Bourdillon and Charles Evans set off for the summit of Everest using a revolutionary closed-circuit oxygen system that recycled exhaled air through a soda lime canister to remove the carbon dioxide, meaning fewer cylinders were required. Initially the men made good progress thanks to their lightweight

Opposite Hillary leads a group into the Western Cwm and towards the infamous Khumbu Icefall.

equipment, but at the South Summit, with just 91m (300ft) to go, Evans' system failed. With a snowstorm brewing, the two exhausted men wisely decided to retreat down the mountain to brief the second assault team of Hillary and Tenzing Norgay.

Blizzards continued throughout the next day, but when the winds eased at dawn on 28 May 1953, the three-man advance party set off to lay equipment dumps higher up the mountain so that Hillary and Norgay could pick up fresh cylinders along the route for their tried-and-tested, but more cumbersome, open-circuit system, which mixed oxygen in the tanks with the ambient air. By mid-afternoon Hillary was carrying more than 27kg (60lb) of oxygen and other essentials needed to summit Everest.

Thoroughly spent, the two men hastily pitched camp on a narrow ledge while the advance party headed back down to the South Col. After checking their equipment Hillary and Norgay tucked into the world's highest picnic, which included sardines, dried biscuits, tinned apricots (from the 'luxury box'), dates and jam, all washed down with soup and lots of hot sweetened lemonade to stave off the effects of dehydration at high altitude.

Despite the high winds they managed four hours' sleep. At around 4.30 a.m. Hillary stuck his head outside the tent to assess the weather only to discover that his boots had frozen solid, as he'd forgotten to place them in his sleeping bag. He had to spend the next two hours thawing them out over the small Primus paraffin camping stove.

By 6.30 a.m. they were ready, and after downing the last of the sardines and biscuits, Hillary and Norgay hoisted the heavy twin-cylindered oxygen systems onto their backs. It was bitterly cold, -27°C (-17°F), but the winds had died down and the skies were now clear. As Hillary noted: 'We knew that the conditions were good enough, so we just made our preparations and pushed on.'

Wearing triple-layered gloves (a leather fingered glove with a mitten outer layer and an inner pair made of silk) and thick down-filled climbing suits, the pair followed in the footsteps of the first assault party up to the South Summit where, just beyond, their final obstacle awaited: a treacherous 15m (50ft) cliff face (now known as the Hillary Step).

'The rock itself, smooth and almost holdless, might have been an interesting Sunday afternoon

EXPEDITIONS UNPACKED

Left Hillary and Norgay wearing the simpler, but much more cumbersome, open-circuit oxygen systems during their ascent of the South East ridge.

Opposite Using ice axes and ropes, and wearing goggles and crampons, the expedition negotiates a treacherous section of the mountain strewn with crevasses.

problem to a group of climbers in the Lake District,' Hillary wrote. 'But here it was a barrier beyond our feeble strength to overcome.'

Spotting a gap between the rock and the ice sticking to the East Face, Hillary wedged himself inside, dug in his crampons and hauled his way to the top, before helping Norgay climb up with a rope. Thoroughly exhausted but with the prize now firmly within their grasp Hillary continued to cut steps into the icy ridge using his forged steel ice axe along a series of frustrating false summits, 'bump after bump, wondering a little desperately where the top could be.'

Eventually, after five hours of hard climbing Hillary noted that: 'the ridge ahead, instead of monotonously rising, now dropped sharply away, and far below, I could see the North Col and the Rongbuk Glacier. I looked upwards to see a narrow snow ridge running up to a snow summit. A few more whacks of the ice axe in the snow and we stood on top.'

The beekeeper from Auckland, and his Nepalese Sherpa companion, had finally conquered Everest, the highest mountain on the planet. Hillary took three photographs of Norgay on the top of Everest

with his Kodak camera. In the snow, Tenzing buried some offerings of food as a gift to the gods, while Hillary laid a small crucifix. After admiring the view and sharing a bar of Kendal Mint Cake they saw that their oxygen was running low and headed back down to the South Col.

At the advanced base camp George Lowe, a fellow Kiwi, welcomed the pair back with mugs of hot soup. Hillary later wrote that his greeting to his team-mate was not specially prepared for public consumption but for Lowe: "Well, we knocked the bastard off!' I told him, and he nodded with pleasure. 'Thought you must have!"

Following his successful ascent of Everest, Hillary became one of the most celebrated and best-known adventurers of the 20th Century. The unassuming New Zealander, however, always acknowledged that the unsung heroes of the expedition were the scientists, engineers and equipment manufacturers that had led a revolution in electronics, oxygen systems and high-performance textiles through the 1940s and 1950s. Without them that 1953 expedition might have become just another failed attempt on the world's highest mountain.

Tim Slessor

Born: c. 1930

Inspired by the Willys Jeep of the Second World War, the first Land Rovers rolled off the Solihull production lines in 1948. They had four-wheel drive, bodywork fashioned from post-war surplus aluminium and a lick of aircraft cockpit paint in varying shades of green. Designed as a light utility vehicle, the basic Land Rover recipe would be used for the next sixty-seven years, producing two million vehicles. In 1955, two of Land Rover's latest Series 1 Station Wagons were donated to the six-man team of the Oxford and Cambridge Far Eastern Expedition for 'field testing' on one of the greatest automotive adventures of all time.

First Overland Unpacked

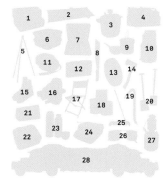

Expedition:
First overland from London to Singapore

Date:
1955

Length:
6 months and 6 days

1. Wooden trunks	15. Terylene socks
2. Camp beds	16. Bell & Howell 70DL camera
3. Pressure cooker 'washing machine'	17. Camping chairs
4. Jerrycans	18. Tinned food
5. Tripod	19. Crowbar
6. Polythene containers	20. Shovels
7. Remington dry shaver	21. Tea
8. Machetes	22. Tape recorder
9. Pots and pans	23. Thermos flasks
10. Rolleiflex camera	24. Typewriter
11. 16mm film	25. Car jack
12. Leica M3 colour camera	26. Sunglasses
13. Dunlop off-road tyres	27. Gas lantern
14. Axe	28. Land Rovers and tents

In 1954, following a drunken bet in a Hong Kong bar, a 40,000km (25,000 mile) trans-African race in Land Rovers had taken place between the rival universities of Oxford and Cambridge. History undergraduate Adrian Cowell had taken the bet on behalf of Cambridge and planned the expedition but, unfortunately, was unable to go. To make matters worse, Oxford won.

The following year, itching for adventure, Cowell hatched an even more audacious plan. Poring over an atlas and drinking coffee late one evening with fellow undergraduate Tim Slessor, he had the idea for a joint university overland expedition to Singapore. As the furthest point east on the Eurasian landmass, several intrepid motorists had tried, but none had succeeded. Thick jungle, parched desert and a worrying lack of roads were realistic concerns Slessor raised.

'Well, no one else has ever done it – so why shouldn't we?' was Cowell's can-do response.

Antony Barrington Brown, better known as B.B., had set up a photographic business after graduating from Cambridge, and became the first to join the team. In the quest for sponsors, B.B. pitched an idea to the head of the BBC's Exploration Unit, where a young David Attenborough gave the team

£200 towards a Bell & Howell 70DL clockwork camera, a tripod and a supply of 16mm film.

Patrick Murphy, a Cambridge geography graduate, secured funds from the Royal Geographical Society and became the team's chief navigator.

Slessor received a £300 advance for a book about the expedition which was added to the kitty, and between them, they badgered and cajoled more than eighty-three companies into supplying them with £8,000 worth of equipment and provisions; everything from Brooke Bond tea to Dunlop off-road tyres, a Grundig tape recorder and their much-loved Terylene socks ('They wash easily, dry quickly, and never need darning').

On 1 September 1955, after a swift pint and a Scotch egg at the Grenadier Pub, just behind Hyde Park Corner, the six-man expedition waved goodbye to TV reporters, family and well-wishers.

Nigel Newberry, the token Oxford man, had applied to join the trip as a 'freelance mechanic' (which simply meant, they later discovered, that he didn't own a car), but was press-ganged into the unenviable role of quartermaster.

Newberry packed away last-minute items in polythene containers and wooden personal trunks

to reduce annoying rattles, wrapping lengths of old rubber inner-tubes around noisy or valuable items. These included two donated still cameras: a black and white Rolleiflex and a Leica M3 colour camera on which 3,000 photographs would be taken over the course of the journey.

The expedition's first major hiccup arose when they reached the Silver Cities Aerodrome just outside London. In the 1950s, car-carrying planes flew out of here every three minutes, but when the Land Rovers reached the top of the aircraft embarkation ramp, they discovered that they were too tall for the Bristol Air Freighter; near disaster was only averted by letting the tyres down and unloading the roof racks.

Landing in France, the first night's camp was in the sand dunes outside Le Touquet, which gave the team a chance to test their ingenious tent system.

Designed to be put up quickly, keep out the rain and allow access to the stowed kit boxes, the canvas roof was attached to the rear of both vehicles and slowly tensioned by driving them apart.

Under here the tensile camp beds were put together; some cleverly placed fittings inside the Land Rovers meant these collapsible beds could also double-up as emergency stretchers. But perhaps the most important piece of equipment, as it is on any British expedition, was the stove on which the tea was brewed. Henry Nott, the team's chief engineer, had opted for a petrol cooker (and lamps) to avoid carrying additional types of fuel; and since Mobil were one of the expedition's key sponsors, that came for free. For tea on the move, the gifted Thermos flasks came in very handy.

In Munich, the Land Rover's engine, gearbox and differential oils were changed, nipples were greased, radiators and batteries topped up, tanks refilled and bodywork scrubbed in less than fourteen minutes by the Mobilgas mechanics. Flat out on the German autobahns the two vehicles – the Oxford one painted a dark blue and the Cambridge one a light blue – reached identical top speeds of 100km/h (62mph), making good time to the Swiss border and on to Vienna.

By the time the Land Rovers had climbed over the pine-covered Austrian Alps into Yugoslavia (now Slovenia), they had been on the road for several days and personal hygiene in the cramped cockpits was already becoming an issue.

Slessor, the only non-bearded team member, made use of the donated Remington dry shaver which ran off the vehicle's 12v electrics, while an ingenious system for washing clothing was designed using a pressure cooker stuffed with dirty clothes, water and soap flakes strapped to the vehicle's floor. It didn't work so well on the 390km (240 miles) of flat concrete roads from Zagreb to Belgrade, but the further east they travelled, as the

Left Stretches of the old Stillwell Road, washed away by decades of monsoon rains, are crudely shored up in the forests of Burma (now Myanmar).

Right Driving alongside a narrow-gauge steam train of the famous Darjeeling Himalayan Railway in India's West Bengal state.

roads began to get worse, the pothole-powered washing machine just got better and better.

Two weeks after leaving London the expedition arrived in Istanbul, where a short ferry ride over the Bosphorus delivered them onto the Asian continent.

The Land Rovers had been designed with these warmer climates in mind with additional air vents and a white-painted, double-skinned Safari Roof, which kept the interior cool. Strapped to the front wings of each vehicle were two 20-litre (4.5 gallon) jerry cans of fresh water (labelled 'Gin' and 'Tonic' on the Oxford car) ready to top up the radiators; to avoid the sun's glare, the drivers wore dark glasses and attached to the top of the Land Rovers' windscreens were large metal visors.

On the gruelling leg across the top of the Syrian Desert, between Damascus and Baghdad, the team devised a primitive form of air conditioning. Noting that: 'it's possible to keep a car quite cool in desert areas by soaking the floor in water, or by hanging wet cloths over open car windows. As the wind blows through the car, it absorbs the moisture, and the temperature drops.' Similarly, wet canvas bags, hung from the outside of the vehicle, chilled the crew's drinking water.

In return for the loan of the two vehicles, the expedition had agreed to showcase the two Land Rover Station Wagons along the route. At a military proving ground near Tehran, a demonstration of the new models' off-road capabilities had been arranged for the Persian General Staff. The Iranian 'Top Brass' were so impressed that they promptly placed an order for one hundred vehicles.

The team spent Christmas 1955 as the guests of Brooke Bond at their Calcutta offices. This was

where the mapped roads ended: to the west lay the jungle-covered foothills of the Himalayas and one of the wettest places on the planet.

Although Burma (now Myanmar) was only 320km (200 miles) away, no permanent road had ever been built between the two countries. However, in one frantic year during the Second World War, the Americans and Chinese worked together, under the command of General 'Vinegar Joe' Stilwell, to hack a 435km (270 mile) 'fighting road' through these mountains where, for just a few months in 1944, thousands of troop carriers and supply trucks trundled across the frontier, chasing the retreating Japanese eastwards. Twelve years on, nobody was sure if the old Stilwell Road was entirely passable or how many bridges had been swept away by a decade of monsoon rains.

There was also the threat of bandits who roamed these mountains, which raised the discussion as to whether the expedition should carry firearms. Some in the team had done their National Service and were handy with a rifle, but the general consensus was that 'a weapon of defence can be very easily mistaken for one of offence', and that by advertising the fact they were carrying arms and ammunition might actually make the vehicles a more attractive prize to a trigger-happy band of robbers. Nevertheless, Newberry took the team's three machetes 'and had them sharpened to a murderous edge'.

Fully laden, each Land Rover weighed in at nearly two tonnes. In preparation for the perilous journey up the steep and slippery Stilwell Road, across the Naga Hills, they decided to lighten the load as much as possible. Surplus pots, pans,

EXPEDITIONS UNPACKED

camping chairs, a Remington typewriter, the less appetising tinned foods and half the team's clothes were jettisoned to make room for road-building essentials including crowbars, hydraulic jacks, shovels and picks.

Sliding and spinning up the misty dirt track, through the appropriately named Hell's Gate, they reached the frontier at the Pangsu Pass, stopping at the border in the pouring rain to make a much-needed brew and settle their jangled nerves.

On the descent into Burma the once well-surfaced two-lane military road deteriorated into a narrow mud trail, as the encroaching jungle brush clattered against the vehicles' sides. In some sections the Land Rovers sank up to their axles, and the team had to slide rafts of bamboo, cut with machetes, under the wheels to provide extra traction. Some stretches of road had been shored up with flimsy bamboo poles, while fallen trees littered the road and had to be cleared with axes and the cars' cable winches.

It was three days of very hard driving before they reached the tarmac of the Burma Road; enduring treacherous mountain roads, fording deep swollen rivers and crossing terrifying rotten bridges, but thankfully, they didn't meet any gun-toting bandits.

By the time the expedition reached Bangkok, the team had been on the road for five months. Only one major geographical hurdle lay ahead: a 160km (100 mile) stretch of the Kra Isthmus.

There were no marked roads here and, initially, a plan had been proposed to bump their way down the east coast railway line. However, the team heard a rumour that an old elephant trail was about to be upgraded and might now be navigable.

The rutted dirt road hugged the palm-fringed coast before it narrowed to a track, which they crept along in bottom gear, through deep rivers, thick bamboo and tangled creepers. After fourteen hours of wading and crawling they were through, and just 1,278km (800 miles) of asphalt roads to Singapore lay ahead. At their camp that night, Brown painted a celebratory 'London-Singapore, First Overland' over the back doors of the Land Rovers – the end was within sight.

On 6 March 1956, escorted over the mile-long causeway by the police and members of the Singapore Auto Club, the Oxford and Cambridge Far Eastern Expedition entered the city, pulling up at the main Rover dealership in Orchard Road after six months and six days on the road and having covered more than 29,000km (18,000 miles).

This record-breaking Boys' Own adventure had only been possible thanks to the generosity of their numerous sponsors. Keeping up their side of the bargain, the team wrote more than eighty articles, and delivered more than 5,680m (10,000ft) of film to the BBC, which produced three TV programmes about the expedition called *Travellers' Tales,* which aired in December 1956.

The subsequent book *The First Overland,* written by Slessor, was published in 1957 and has become a classic among armchair automotive adventurers. As Sir David Attenborough recounted in the foreword of the fiftieth anniversary edition, the only reason you shouldn't gift a copy to your loved one is that they: 'Will almost certainly then want a Land Rover for Christmas.' He was right ...

TIM SLESSOR

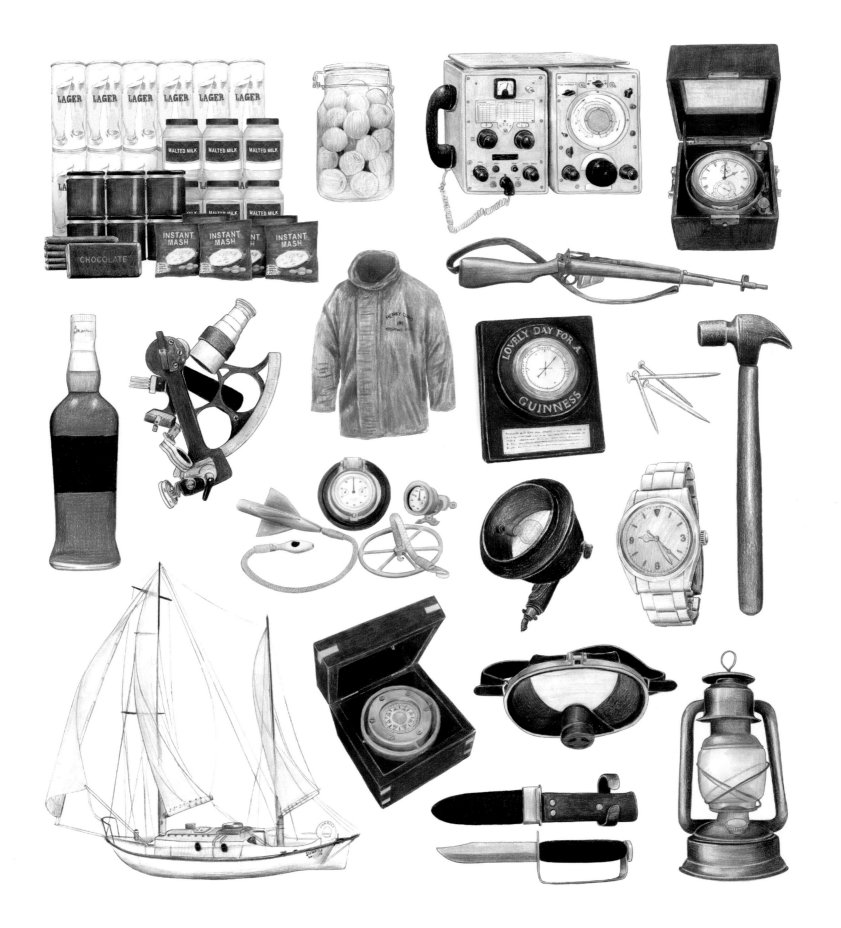

Sir Robin Knox-Johnston

Born: 17 March 1939, UK

On 28 May 1968, British yachtsman Francis Chichester became the first man to sail solo around the world aboard *Gipsy Moth IV.* He became a British hero and an inspiration to generations of sailors who would follow in his wake. In the sailing world, there was now only one great challenge left: to sail single-handed, non-stop around the globe. In March 1968, the *Sunday Times* announced the Golden Globe Race for the plucky few adventurers that were brave enough to try. One man who stepped up was twenty-nine-year-old Merchant Navy Officer Robin Knox-Johnston.

Sunday Times Golden Globe Unpacked

Expedition:
Non-stop, solo expedition, sailing around the world

Date:
1968–1969

Length:
312 days

1. Food supplies including 120 cans of lager
2. Pickled onions
3. Radio transmitter
4. Wind-up chronometer
5. Rifle
6. Whisky
7. Sextant
8. Oilskins
9. Novelty barometer
10. Nails
11. Hammer
12. Walker trailing log
13. Signal lamp
14. Rolex wristwatch
15. Suhaili Bermudan ketch
16. Compass
17. Diver's goggles
18. Diver's knife
19. Hurricane lamp

Opposite A pristine-looking *Suhaili* photographed from the air shortly after leaving Falmouth at the start of the 1968 Golden Globe Race.

Built of Indian teak, *Suhaili* was a sturdy 10m (32ft) long Bermudan ketch – a sailboat with two masts: a main mast and a shorter 'missin mast' further back. Robin Knox-Johnston had constructed the ketch himself in a Bombay dockyard in 1963, to a design used for Norwegian sailing lifeboats. As he himself admitted 'she was no greyhound' compared to the faster sloops and trimarans taking part.

Heavily laden with a tonne of tinned food and various British delicacies (including Cadbury's chocolate, Horlicks, Bovril, Smash instant potato and 120 cans of donated Tennent's Lager), the *Suhaili* sat worryingly low in the water at Falmouth Harbour as last-minute preparations were made.

There was no entry fee, and virtually no rules nor qualification requirements for the Golden Globe Race. Nine entrants signed up for the challenge, with varying degrees of experience, and in an eclectic assortment of sailing boats. Entrants were allowed to set off from any point of the British Isles, at anytime between 1 June and 31 October 1968, to ensure they reached the treacherous Southern Ocean in the summer months.

The British yachtsman John Ridgeway, in the sloop *English Rose IV*, was the first to set off, leaving Inishmore on the west of Ireland on the first possible day. The firm favourite to take the Golden Globe trophy for being the first to complete an unassisted circumnavigation of the globe, and the £5,000 prize pot for setting the fastest time, however, was the celebrated French sailor and maritime author Bernard Moitessier in his custom-built steel-hulled ketch, *Joshua*.

In stark contrast, the least experienced competitor was the Scotsman Chay Blyth, who had rowed the Atlantic but had absolutely no sailing experience whatsoever. He had to get some sailing chums to help rig his 9m (30ft) sloop *Dytiscus* and when he cast off from the banks of the River Hamble, a week after Ridgeway, they sailed out ahead of him in another yacht to demonstrate the basics.

Although Knox-Johnston had plenty of experience, having sailed the *Suhaili* to India just a few years before, he was still a rank outsider – in fact, few folk thought that his chances of winning, in his sluggish wooden sailboat, were much better than Blyth's.

Knox-Johnston's voyage began on 14 June 1968. Despite the old maritime superstition that beginning a voyage on a Friday brings bad luck, he made a good start and was quickly gaining on the other two competitors as they approached the equator in early August. The last starters got away by late October with Moitessier setting a tremendous pace; covering 350km (188 nautical miles) in one day's sailing, the Frenchman in his lightweight sloop was almost twice as fast as Knox-Johnston over the same course.

As the *Suhaili* entered the South Atlantic she began to take on water. To make emergency repairs Knox-Johnston would have to freedive beneath and caulk the gaps between the planks near her keel – not an easy task without breathing apparatus, below a rocking sailboat and with a large blue shark lingering off your bow. With his tools, diver's knife and goggles to hand, Knox-Johnston dropped some sheets of toilet paper onto the water, and as the shark popped up to investigate, he raised his .303 Lee-Enfield rifle and fired, killing the prowling predator stone dead. Four hours later the leaks were sealed and he was back in the race.

Around a thousand kilometres off the South African coast, the sailboat was battered by a series of storms driven by ferocious force 10 gales. One night, as Knox-Johnston slept, the boat was hit by a huge wave, which threw him from his bunk and almost capsized the boat. As it righted itself, he scrabbled around for the hurricane lamp to inspect the damage only to find seawater streaming into the cabin and onto the chart table. When the next wave pounded the side of the boat, with a sickening crunch, the cabin was almost torn off its fixings. Crawling onto deck in his oilskins he found that

Right Robin Knox-Johnston at the helm of his 9.8m (32ft) Bermudan ketch *Suhaili*. Built from sturdy Indian teak, 'she was no greyhound' compared to the other entrants' vessels.

Left With his radio knocked out of action Knox-Johnston finally made contact with a passing merchant ship after 21 weeks at sea to let his family know that he was safe and still in the race.

the steel tubing of the boat's self-steering gear had been damaged beyond repair. Knox-Johnston hadn't realised just how close the boat had been to completely flipping over until he later found a coin caught in a cabin roof beam.

More worryingly, the near-capsize had knocked out his Marconi Kestrel radio transmitter. Unable to update race HQ about his whereabouts, concerns for his safety grew back home. This also meant he was no longer able to get time checks

via the onshore stations to ensure his wind-up chronometer and Rolex Explorer wristwatch were a hundred per cent accurate – something that was absolutely crucial when navigating by sextant. The only other navigational aids he had to help plot his progress were the ship's compass and a Walker trailing log, which calculated the boat's approximate speed.

Without a radio Knox-Johnston was also unable to get weather updates and was forced to make

rough forecasts using general observations and a novelty barometer that he had borrowed from a pub, bearing the slogan: 'A lovely day for a Guinness.' In the Southern Ocean, it rarely was.

Between Cape Town and New Zealand the storms were relentless – the impact of the waves were: 'like someone swinging an anvil against the hull', Knox-Johnston recalled.

Although he had managed to secure the cabin roof with a hammer and nails, some sails had been torn, the main gooseneck (the swivel that connects the boom to the main mast) was damaged and 70 litres (15 gallons) of fresh water in the boat's storage tanks had become polluted. For the rest of the journey Knox-Johnston would have to rely on rainwater collected in his sails to recharge his tanks.

On the 147th day Knox-Johnston made contact with a merchant vessel using his signal lamp and passed on some mail to say that all was well. Although he'd remembered stationery, three things Knox-Johnston had forgotten to pack in the pre-race excitement were razors for shaving, the pump for the compressed air spear gun and solder for repairing electronics. In a desperate bid to mend the frazzled radio he came up with an ingenious bodge, melting the bottoms of his spare navigation light bulbs to collect the liquid metal. The set was eventually fixed just in time to receive an urgent message from a *Sunday Mirror* journalist who was following his progress, urging him to drop anchor outside Bluff Harbour on New Zealand's South Island, and ride out the viscous

EXPEDITIONS UNPACKED

squall that was heading his way. Sailing through the night, Knox-Johnston headed towards the coast as advised, where, much to his embarrassment, he ran aground. Fortunately, this wasn't to be the end of his race; with no damage done, and only five hours lost, the rules clearly stipulated that he would only be disqualified if he were to go ashore.

Knox-Johnston's supporters in New Zealand reckoned that Moitessier, his closest rival, was around 6,400km (4,000 miles) behind; even though the *Joshua* was a much faster vessel, this still gave him a fighting chance of reaching home before the Frenchman. On Christmas Day, feeling optimistic about his chances, he celebrated with one of the twelve bottles of whisky and a jar of pickled onions he had stowed on board, held a rousing solo carol service, and, at the customary time of 3 p.m., drank a toast to Her Majesty the Queen.

By the time the *Suhaili* rounded the tip of South America at Cape Horn on 17 January 1969, five of the nine starters had retired due to the mental pressures, illness or technical problems. What Knox-Johnston couldn't know was that Moitessier was having second thoughts about the whole endeavour too, eventually firing a message in a tin can to a passing ship near Cape Town, announcing

that: 'My intention is to continue the voyage, still non-stop, toward the Pacific Islands, where there is plenty of sun and more peace than in Europe.'

Retiring from the race he continued sailing *Joshua* eastwards to Tahiti, to rest up and 'save his soul' as he put it.

With the two faster trimarans gaining on the old teak ketch, the bookmakers' predictions were for Knox-Johnston to narrowly take the trophy while the two remaining English yachtsmen, David Crowhurst and Nigel Tetley, were equal favourites in the race for the 'fastest circumnavigation' prize.

Crowhurst had left Devon on the last possible start date, 31 October 1968, aboard the fast, but largely untested, three-hulled *Teignmouth Electron*. Built to Crowhurst's exacting specifications, the high-tech trimaran was twice over budget, and hastily completed only days before the race's deadline. Because many safety features were not fully fitted, and there was just a tangle of coloured wires where the start-of-the-art navigational computer was supposed to be, Crowhurst estimated, in his personal log, that he had only a fifty per cent chance of surviving the race. With sponsors, book and TV deals secured, he was faced with the difficult choice of either pulling out and

facing financial ruin and humiliation, or risking his life in an unseaworthy experimental boat.

Over the next two months, as equipment failed and design flaws became apparent, the hopelessness of his situation led him to a desperate act of deception as he began falsifying his navigational logs and location transmissions. Loitering off the coast of South America for several months, Crowhurst's plan was to rejoin the race as the other competitors returned to the South Atlantic, at the back of the pack as a mere runner-up, but with his reputation intact.

On 22 April 1969, rank outsider Knox-Johnston, in his self-built wooden ketch, sailed into Falmouth amid a flotilla of well-wishers sounding their horns. After 30,000 miles and 312 days at sea he became the first person to single-handedly circumnavigate the world non-stop, and the winner of the *Sunday Times* Golden Globe trophy.

Meanwhile, out in the Atlantic, Tetley, believing he was still in a neck-and-neck race with Crowhurst, pushed his weather-beaten trimaran *Victress* to breaking point, eventually having to abandon ship just 2,037km (1,100 nautical miles)

from his home port of Plymouth.

This meant that Crowhurst, who had set off four and a half months after Knox-Johnston, was almost certain to take the £5,000 prize for fastest time, which would expose his navigational logs to intense scrutiny by the press and race officials. Unable to see any way out of his predicament, and wracked with guilt after Tetley's sinking, Crowhurst took his own life, jumping overboard into the Atlantic Ocean in July 1969. On hearing this tragic news Knox-Johnston asked for his 'fastest time' prize money to be donated to Crowhurst's widow.

Knighted for his services to yacht racing, Knox-Johnston never tired of exploring the open seas: in 1994 he set a new record for the fastest circumnavigation of the world, and in 2007 sailed solo around the globe to take a commendable fourth place in the Velux 5 Ocean Race, aged sixty-eight years old.

As the winner of the Golden Globe Race of 1968–69, he accomplished 'the sailing equivalent of climbing Mount Everest' and 'perhaps the last great uncomputerised journey left to man'.

Opposite The crew of a Royal Navy vessel welcome Knox-Johnston back to the English south coast as he nears the end of his record-breaking non-stop circumnavigation.

Above left Knox-Johnston downs a long-awaited pint of beer in celebration as he comes ashore at Falmouth Harbour on 22 April 1969.

Above right Knox-Johnston raising his arms in triumph as he struggles to regain his 'land legs' after 312 days at sea.

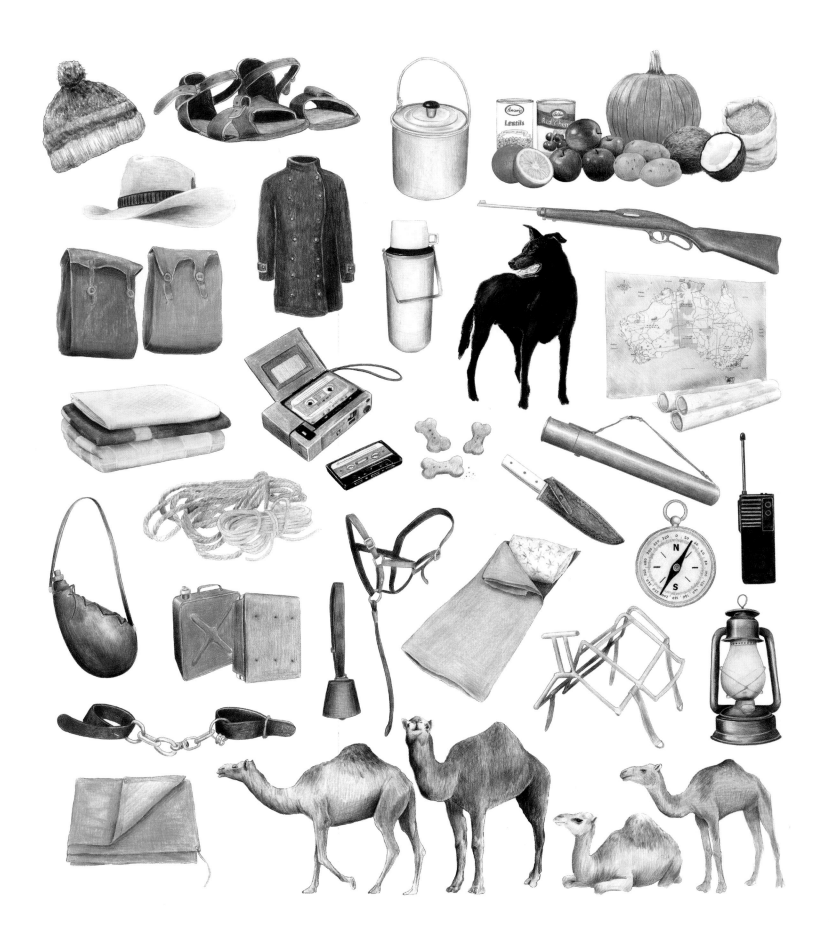

Robyn Davidson

Born: 6 September 1950, Australia

In 1975 Robyn Davidson arrived in Alice Springs with a dog, AUS$6, a 'suitcase full of inappropriate clothes' and the 'lunatic idea' of training a team of camels for a 2,740km (1,700 mile) trek from Australia's central desert to the shores of the Indian Ocean. For two years she worked and trained on the local camel farms, scrimping and saving for her journey, eventually accepting sponsorship from *National Geographic* to purchase the supplies and equipment she needed to embark on a journey through one of the most inhospitable places on planet Earth.

Western Australia
Expedition Unpacked

Expedition:
Trek across the deserts of west Australia using camels

Date:
1977

Length:
9 months

1. Woolly hat
2. Sandals
3. Billie cans
4. Food supplies
5. Hat
6. Canvas and leather kit bags
7. Raincoat
8. Thermos flask
9. Davidson's dog Diggity
10. Rifle
11. Maps of Australia
12. Mosquito nets
13. Ropes
14. Portable cassette player
15. Dog biscuits
16. Belt knife
17. Map carrier
18. Compass
19. Two-way radio
20. Goatskin water canteens
21. Water drums
22. Camel bells
23. Camel harness
24. Swag (sleeping bag)
25. Camel saddles
26. Kerosene lamp
27. Camel leg straps
28. Orange plastic raincoats
29. Dookie
30. Bub
31. Zeleika
31. Goliath

EXPEDITIONS UNPACKED

Left Robyn Davidson heads into the outback with her four camels, her faithful dog Diggity and 680kg (1,500lbs) of equipment for her 2,736km (1,700 mile) trek across Western Australia.

After finishing at her girls' boarding school in Brisbane, Robyn Davidson lived a bohemian life in Sydney, quitting university, she worked as a blackjack dealer in an illegal gambling den and as a part-time artist's model. Before she reached the outback she had 'never held a hammer … mended a sock, changed a tyre, or used a screwdriver', and yet nothing would shake her from her grand plan to walk halfway across Australia.

In March 1977, aged twenty-six years old, Davidson set out on the first leg of her life-changing journey from Glen Helen camp, 100km (60 miles) west of Alice Springs, with her team of four camels, her faithful dog Diggity and 680kg (1,500lb) of equipment and provisions loaded onto three steel-framed saddles cushioned with leather pads stuffed with straw. The two bulls, Dookie and Bub, carried most of the burden, with each camel carrying four drums of fresh water, weighing 23kg (50lb) each, and various canvas and leather kit bags. Zeleika, who was still feeding her young calf Goliath, carried a lighter load, which included the goatskin water canteens, spare ropes, tools and harnesses.

The first trial run was a 27km (17 mile) trek to Redbank Gorge; this was an opportunity to sort out last-minute snags with equipment, and for *National Geographic* photographer Rick Smolan to grab some action shots of the expedition's outset.

Smolan's new Toyota 4x4 was loaded to the gunwales with every survival gadget and gizmo that the salesmen in Melbourne could convince him he would need to cross the desert: 'from a winch the size of a bull to a rubber dinghy with paddles that took half an hour to inflate.'

Smolan insisted that Davidson should take a two-way radio with her. 'It didn't feel right. I didn't need it … didn't want that mental crutch, or physical link with the outside world.' Eventually, however, she relented, but refused the huge pedal-powered generator that Smolan had brought too.

The plan had been to follow the old trackway from here to Areyonga, a tiny missionary station nestled in the MacDonnell Ranges. Strapped to the side of Bub's riding saddle was a cylindrical tube containing the 1:250,000 topographical maps which, along with the compass her father had given her, were Davidson's only means of navigation.

However, she soon discovered that the government maps could not be relied upon, as marked paths got swallowed up by sandy creeks, stopped at some long-forgotten bore well or

Right Davidson consults one of her woefully inaccurate 1:250,000 topographical maps.

Opposite top Wherever Davidson and her camel train went, the local indigenous children greeted them with tremendous excitement.

Opposite bottom left After making camp Davidson would drift off to sleep listening to teaching tapes on her portable cassette player that helped her to learn Pitjantjatjara, the local indigenous dialect.

Opposite bottom right Davidson, lying between two camels, reading a paperback. Just one of the many photographs taken by *National Geographic* cameraman Rick Smolan.

branched off into countless animal tracks. Angry and frustrated, Davidson became convinced that cartographers, surveying from the air, must 'have been drunk at the time; or perhaps just felt like breaking free of departmental rulings and added a few bits and pieces of imaginative topography, or even, in some cases, rubbed out a few.'

They covered just 32km (20 miles) on that second day. Camping by the side of the trail, Davidson lit kerosene lamps, unfurled mosquito nets and built brushwood campfires to 'boil up the billies' for that first night's meal. She was apprehensive about her first night alone, out in the bush, not because she was scared of the dark, or overly concerned about the poisonous snakes, scorpions or the vicious 20cm (8in) millipedes that liked to sleep under the swag (sleeping bag), but because she was worried her beloved camels would wander off in the night.

To limit their movements, but still allow them the freedom to graze, the adult camels were hobbled with leg straps, hung with little bells, attached to a 12m (40ft rope). Once they were settled and secure, Davidson settled down for the night, drifting off to sleep while listening to indigenous language learning tapes on her portable cassette player.

When she woke up the next morning, Diggity was under her blankets and the four camels were huddled around the swag – initially, it seemed, they were more afraid of the outback than she was.

The morning routine was quickly established: boiling a couple of billies over the rekindled campfire and filling the Thermos with sweetened tea, before the arduous task of reloading the saddles began, carefully balancing the load as each item was stowed. Dookie, the strongest bull, carried the large hessian sack of provisions, including fruit, lentils, brown rice, potatoes, coconuts and pumpkins. To supplement her diet, indigenous Australian friends had taught Davidson the basics of bush tucker survival, and she always kept a knife on her belt ready to cut down kakadu plums (containing a hundred times more Vitamin C than an orange) or to dig out a nutritious witchetty grub from the trunk of a fallen gum tree.

After three days of solitude, the cheering throngs of children as Davidson arrived in Areyonga were a welcome surprise. With her water bags refilled, the village elders warned that the route from here over the mountains towards Uluru, 240km (150 miles) to the southwest, was an old one, unused for many years. It was difficult navigation for the next couple

ROBYN DAVIDSON

EXPEDITIONS UNPACKED

of weeks, as Davidson 'sweated over compass and map' through vast expanses of shifting red sand, dotted with desert oaks.

In the 1970s, most camels were controlled by the use of nose pegs. This practice had been used for centuries and involved a piece of wood, shaped like a bishop from a chess set, being attached to the inside of the camel's nostrils.

Many of these camels came from Afghanistan and India with their handlers in the 1840s to help build the telegraph system and eventually the railways. Once the work was complete, they were released into the wild where they adapted easily to their new surroundings. When Davidson was trekking in 1977 there were around 10,000 wild camels in the Australian outback. Today, the population is closer to 1.2 million.

Twenty-one days, and 400km (250 miles), after leaving Glen Helen, Davidson reached Uluru where she met up again with Smolan from the *National Geographic*, who clicked away with his Nikon to get the obligatory shot of the camels trekking in front of this great sacred monolith.

Despite the hoards of tourists, Uluru didn't disappoint: 'surrounded by fertile flats for a radius of half a mile which, because of the added run-off water, were covered in lush green feed and wildflowers so thick you couldn't step between them.'

They made camp at the Olgas, a lesser-known collection of thirty-six huge ochre-coloured rock domes, 32km (20 miles) to the west and away from inquisitive tourists.

The next 225km (140 mile) leg to the Docker River started well, but then the weather turned. The camels, with their broad soft pads, did not cope well with the slippery mud paths; nor were they fond of the plastic raincoats, which Davidson had designed to keep the packs dry, flapping about in the wind.

After sixty-nine days on the move the camel train reached the Gibson Desert. Davidson's Afghani camel guru in Alice Springs had given her some sage advice regarding the wild camels they were likely to encounter at this stage in the trip: 'Make no mistake, wild bull camels can kill you when they're in rut. They will try to take a female, and if you are in the way, you'll be attacked. The only thing that will stop them is a bullet. If the time should come, don't hesitate.'

One hundred and eighty metres (200yd) ahead stood three wild bulls with their horny 'come-hither' eyes trained firmly on Zeleika – it seemed that the time had come. Slowly sliding her Savage 0.222 over-under rifle from its scabbard on Bub's saddle, Davidson trained her sights on the nearest bull. As it began to close in she had no choice but to dispatch it with three quick rounds; as the leader fell, the others wisely scattered.

Through the Gibson Desert, water supplies ran perilously low; thankfully, the artesian wells marked on the maps were more or less where they should have been. As food also ran low Davidson shared the tinned dog biscuits with Diggity, until the indigenous people she met on the Gunbarrel Highway replenished her supplies.

This arrow-straight mix of gravel, dirt and flood-plains ran for 1,350km (840 miles) to Carnegie Station in Western Australia, and was originally built as part of Australia's nuclear weapons testing programme in the 1950s. In 1977, a six-wheeled truck passed along this road every two months; it was remote, but easily navigable, following the two parallel wheel ruts to the Canning Stock Road.

It was here that Davidson put on her last pair of leather strapped sandals. Boots had proved too heavy; running shoes didn't breathe and collected ridges of sand under the balls of her feet. But by this stage the animals' feet were suffering, too – Dookie had an improvised leather boot, fashioned by a kindly passing motorist, to try and protect his injured pad; and when Diggity's paws became sore from the spinifex prickles, she hitched a lift on Bub.

The Canning Stock Road marked the beginning of the end – only a relatively easy 725km (450 miles) to the Indian Ocean remained. The road to Wiluna was dotted with watering holes of varying quality: 'Well No.6 hardly deserved the name. The surface of the water lay nine feet below ground level and could only be reached with a bucket, a rope and enough effort to cause a hernia. The

Above 'The camels simply couldn't comprehend so much water. They would stare at it, walk a few paces, then turn and stare again.

Opposite 195 days after leaving Glen Helen, near Alice Springs, Davidson and her camels enjoy a dip in the Indian Ocean.

water tasted foul, but none of us cared, and I camouflaged mine with huge doses of coffee.'

It was here, between the water stops, that tragedy struck. This was dingo country, and while off scavenging one evening, Diggity took a poisoned bait, laid out by a local landowner, and died in Davidson's arms. Davidson was distraught, but pragmatic: 'My only thought now was to push on to the end of my route. The country passed unnoticed beneath my feet, and I recall little of that time.'

As her journey neared the ocean, and the road networks improved, more and more journalists from all over the world were dispatched to the outback to photograph and interview the 'Camel Lady', as she was now internationally known.

She was asked countless times to explain why she did it, and her answer was pretty straightforward: 'I love the desert and its incomparable sense of space. I enjoy being with Aborigines and learning from them. I like the freedom inherent in being on my own, and I like the growth and learning processes that develop from taking chances. And, obviously, camels are the best means of getting across deserts.'

One-hundred-and-ninety-five days after leaving Glen Helen, Smolan caught the final push to the coast on camera. His photographs of Davidson's camels ambling in the surf became famous across the globe. As Davidson later wrote: 'The camels simply couldn't comprehend so much water. They would stare at it, walk a few paces, then turn and stare again. Dookie pretended he wasn't scared, but his eyes were popping out and his ears were so erect they pulled his eyelashes back.'

Davidson's subsequent book, *Tracks*, has never been out of print, was adapted into an award-winning film in 2013, and has been an inspiration to legions of desert adventurers. In it she writes: 'The two important things that I learned from the trip were that you are as powerful and strong as you allow yourself to be, and that the most difficult part of any endeavour is taking the first step.'

Sir Ranulph Fiennes

Born: 7 March 1944, UK

Sir Ranulph Twisleton-Wykeham-Fiennes, 3rd Baronet, might have inherited a title and long ancestral history, but in 1972 the ex-SAS officer was earning a living writing and giving talks about his various adventures across the globe. In 1969, Fiennes had led a team up the White Nile by hovercraft, and in 1971 made the first north to south crossing of Canada by inland waterway. But in 1972, over a simmering pot of Irish stew in the kitchen of their London home, Fiennes' wife, Ginny, suggested they attempt one of the most ambitious round-the-world adventures of all time: the first circumpolar navigation of the globe.

Transglobe Expedition Unpacked

Expedition:
Transglobe

Date:
1979–1982

Length:
2 years 2 months

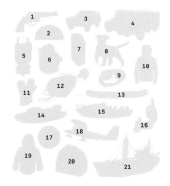

1. Revolver
2. Inclinometer
3. Station wagon
4. Land Rovers
5. Theodolite
6. Cine camera
7. Jerrycans
8. Jack Russell terrier
9. Ski goggles
10. Duck down jackets
11. Mittens
12. Snowmobile
13. Canoes
14. Dunlop rubber boats
15. Fibreglass-hulled Boston Whaler
16. Hand compass
17. Aneroid barometer
18. De Havilland Twin Otter aircraft
19. Eskimo wolfskin parkas
20. Insulated cardboard huts
21. Benjamin Bowring

EXPEDITIONS UNPACKED

For seven years, working out of a windowless office above a disused rifle range, Ranulph Fiennes and a team of unpaid volunteers secured permissions, visas and over 700 sponsors to provide everything from underpants to frozen fish for their ambitious Transglobe expedition.

While government bureaucrats were reluctant to rubber stamp a journey through politically sensitive regions of the South Pole, Prince Charles thought the whole venture was 'mad, but marvellous', and became the expedition's patron.

The first hurdle was securing an ocean-going vessel to serve as the expedition's floating sea base; one that was capable of navigating the polar pack ice, carrying 100 tonnes of provisions and accommodating thirty-six crew members (plus Bothie, the Jack Russell terrier). Eventually, the shipping company C.T. Bowring & Co. (the one-time owners of Captain Scott's *Terra Nova*) agreed to help. The 65m (213ft) *Benjamin Bowring* was a thirty-year-old icebreaker with 2.5cm (1in) thick plating on the bow, a powerful diesel engine capable of 20km/h (11 knots) and state-of-the-art navigational equipment.

On 2 September 1979, Prince Charles skippered the '*Benji Bee*' – as it was nicknamed – away from Greenwich Pier in London amid a fanfare of ships'

horns and waving well-wishers before disembarking at Tilbury Docks, 30km (20 miles) further down the river.

Meanwhile, Fiennes and his two land-team members, Oliver Shepard and Charlie Burton, set off to drive the expedition's vehicles across Europe.

Land Rover had generously supplied the expedition with two Series III station wagons (one containing the radio and a 2.75m (9ft) whip antenna mounted to the rear) and a Range Rover, each pulling a single-axle trailer.

After the 1,600km (1,000 mile) slog south, the vehicles rejoined the *Benji Bee* at the Spanish coast and were hoisted aboard for the short hop across the Mediterranean Sea.

Following the 0° line of longitude, the team headed due south from the port of Algiers towards Tabenkort in Mali, a similar trans-Saharan route pioneered by the Swedish automotive adventurer, Eva Dickson, in 1932.

To escape the high humidity of the Algerian coast, the desert driving stints began at 5 a.m. each day. In the punishing 38°C (100°F) heat of the Sahara Desert, water was rationed to 4.5 litres (1 gallon) per day from the vehicles' jerrycans (a German Second World War design with stamped indentations on the sides that allowed for expansion

EXPEDITIONS UNPACKED

in the heat). Sandstorms were frequent, lasting up to three hours at a time, but the team took no rest during the day, only breaking to make camp at around 5 p.m. each evening – before it got too dark to spot the scorpions and spiders underfoot.

Eventually, barren desert gave way to tropical forests and the lush coastal strip of the Ivory Coast where the faithful *Benji Bee* awaited them in the port of Abidjan. When the ship set sail for Antarctica on 22 November 1979 the expedition's de Havilland Twin Otter support aircraft was undergoing final checks back in the UK before its long flight south. It had taken two months to convert the twenty-seat commercial aircraft into a long-range cargo shuttle capable of the 21,000km (13,000 mile) hop down to the landing strip at Sanae in Queen Maud Land, Antarctica.

The ship's crew spent Christmas 1979 in the 'Roaring Forties' (the area between the latitudes of 40° and 50° south of the equator that is renowned for strong winds), battered by giant waves. At one point, the *Benji Bee* rocked over to 47°, according to the ship's inclinometer: the very same brass instrument that was carried aboard Captain Robert

Scott's *Discovery*, a relic from the heroic age of Antarctic exploration.

The *Benji Bee* carved its way through the Antarctic pack ice, until in early January 1980, it could go no further and the backbreaking job of unloading the cargo onto the sea ice began. Using a fleet of snowmobiles, 100 tonnes of food, provisions and equipment, and more than 100 drums of aviation fuel were ferried 3km (2 miles) across the ice to the onshore airstrip, where the Twin Otter would begin transporting supplies to depots inland.

Keen to avoid the fate that befell some of Scott's ponies – and falling through the pack ice – the team worked quickly; but before they could get the last loads ashore, the winds rose and the pack ice began to break up. Fiennes' team could do nothing but watch as eight drums of aircraft fuel and the chief engineer's motorbike drifted off on an ice floe.

The three-man overland team of Fiennes, Shephard and Burton began their Antarctic crossing on 25 January 1980, leaving the Sanae base on Ski-Doos. Behind each Ski-Doo were two fully laden sledges, built from special steel and coated in

Right Flying both British and American flags, in recognition of the support given to Transglobal by the Amundsen-Scott South Pole Station, the Ski-Doos of Oliver Shepard, Ranulph Fiennes and Charlie Burton are led by a dog team and sledge.

non-stick Teflon. However, this amount of metal in proximity to the magnetic compass made navigation difficult. Remembering an old army trick, used on Land Rovers in the desert, Fiennes scored a series of lines into the windshield and front cowling of his Ski-Doo to create an improvised sun compass. Navigating on the go kept the sledges moving, saving time and putting less strain on the Ski-Doos' troublesome driveshafts; the team stopped only when necessary to check their exact position using the theodolite and aneroid barometer.

Even now, with 24-hour sunlight, the three men had to wrap up against the biting polar winds, wearing five layers of clothing topped off with thick duck down jackets or traditional Inuit wolfskin parkas similar to those used by Roald Amundsen's men in 1913. Eyes were protected by tinted ski goggles and hands were covered with thick insulated Inuit-style mittens to stop them freezing up on the Ski-Doo's hand throttles.

More than once the Ski-Doos would buck over a snow ridge, and the team would look back and see mile-deep cracks open up behind them. At one point, stopping to film the other two snowmobiles,

the leg of Fiennes' monopod went through a thin crust of snow to reveal a crevasse the height of St. Paul's Cathedral. 'With a feeling I remembered so well from Arabia, treading where antipersonnel mines were suspected, I retreated as though barefoot on hot bricks.'

Part of the team had flown 370km (230 miles) further south in the Twin Otter to Borga and established a base of huts made from insulated cardboard buried deep in the snow. The overland team joined the others here and they waited out the vicious polar winter for the next eight months; sheltered from the 145km/h (90mph) winds and a wind-chill factor of -82°C (-116°F), which could freeze human flesh in less than thirty seconds.

By the end of October 1980 there was enough light for the three-man team to set out on their Ski-Doos for the American Amundsen-Scott South Pole Station. Like Scott's *Terra Nova* expedition, Transglobal had been conducting a range of scientific duties since leaving Greenwich; in Africa the Natural History Museum had requested they collect little-known bat and lizard specimens, and from their winter base, Shephard had broadcast

meteorological reports every six hours. Out here on the ice sheet the team now took ice-core samples to study Antarctic snowfall – while the crew of the *Benji Bee*, now in warmer climes, undertook a wide range of oceanographic research.

On 15 December 1980, the Ski-Doos reached the South Pole base, where Fiennes was reunited with his wife, Ginny, and her dog, Bothie. Enjoying a few days' rest the Brits took on the Americans for a friendly game of cricket in full polar gear at -42°C (-44°F). The next leg over to the Ross Ice Shelf was through a more familiar region of Antarctica, running close to the routes used by Scott and Amundsen in 1913.

Fiennes' 67-day crossing of Antarctica by Ski-Doo was to set a new world record for crossing the continent, arriving at the eerily preserved remains of Scott's Hut six weeks ahead of schedule. 'We felt, I think, a silent affinity with our dead countrymen, their journeys long done, ours only half completed.'

On 19 January 1981, the *Benji Bee* broke through the ice floes with Land of Hope and Glory blaring from the ship's loudspeakers. Sailing north, via New Zealand and Australia, it made its way

up the North American coast, towards Alaska, anchoring near the mouth of the Yukon delta in late June 1981. Fiennes and Burton, aboard two 3.65m (12ft) rubber boats, soon found that the Yukon's currents and crosswinds were too much for their tiny craft. Instead, they exited the river at Yukon Bridge after 240km (150 miles) and took the long drive up the Dempster Highway by Land Rover to Tuktoyaktuk, the gateway to the Northwest Passage, where they switched to a 5.5m (18ft) fibreglass-hulled Boston Whaler.

Amid the notorious sea fogs of this treacherous waterway, through an area where magnetic compasses were notoriously unreliable, Fiennes navigated by a 'Zoomski'. Named after the British Aerospace apprentice who invented it, this device could monitor subtle variations in solar radiation, even in a whiteout, to determine the direction of the sun within 15° accuracy. It worked well – Fiennes noted that the shores of the Northwest Passage were littered with the wrecks of those who had not had the benefit of such a gadget.

Reaching Tanquary Fjord on 31 August 1981, the pair trekked overland for four weeks through

the icy rock fields of Canada's Ellesmere Island towards Alert, the northernmost permanently inhabited settlement on Earth. Spotting a chance for some free cold-weather testing, the Army Mountain and Arctic Warfare Committee had provided calorie-rich ration packs, while other manufacturers donated breathable Ventile parkas, Gore-Tex jackets and Canadian Army canvas boots for this long overland yomp.

After wintering at Alert for five months, waiting for the summer sun to return, the pair left for the North Pole on 12 February 1982, beginning their journey on Ski-Doo, before walls of broken ice and fractured ice floes slowed their progress to a painful crawl. A back-up plan involved the delivery of two aluminium canoes, which could be man-hauled over the ice and paddled over water. Fiennes agreed with most polar experts that dog teams might have been a better option, but recognised that Amundsen's brutal 'dog-eat-dog' fuelling strategy would have been a total PR disaster.

Back on the Ski-Doos, with 100km (60 miles) to go, the pair began to pick up speed as a cold snap refroze the ice floes to a solid mass. On

Easter Sunday 1982, they radioed the *Benji Bee* to report they were at 90° north. Planting a Union Flag in the ever-shifting ice over the North Pole, Fiennes and Burton congratulated each other on being the first men to reach both ends of the Earth 'the hard way', before celebrating with 'a nicely chilled magnum'.

The next day the Twin Otter flew out to meet them with members of the expedition including Bothie, who became the first dog to visit both poles. By the end of April 1982, unseasonably warm temperatures caused the frozen seas to break up and the pair spent an unnerving ninety-nine days adrift on a crumbling floe (including a visit from a polar bear that had to be encouraged to 'shove off' with a .44 Ruger revolver). Eventually, on 3 August 1982, the *Benjamin Bowring* plucked them from the ice.

On 29 August 1982, the Transglobal Expedition sailed back up the Thames to a cheering crowd of 10,000 people. It had successfully circumnavigated the planet through its polar axis – an unequalled feat that earned Fiennes recognition in the *Guinness Book of Records* as the 'World's Greatest Living Explorer'.

Above Fiennes loads his .44 Ruger revolver; an item of equipment that proved very useful in the Arctic for encouraging inquisitive polar bears to 'shove off'.

Left Shepard, Fiennes and Burton stand in front of Captain Scott's hut. Untouched until 1956, when US explorers rediscovered it and dug it out of the ice, New Zealand and the UK now take joint responsibility for its preservation.

Reinhold Messner

Born: 17 September 1944, Italy

There are fourteen mountain peaks on Earth that rise above 8,000m (26,000ft), all within the Himalayan and Karakoram ranges of Central Asia. In October 1986, the Tyrolean climber Reinhold Messner became the first person to summit them all. He was also the first man to make a solo ascent of Mount Everest. Described by many as the greatest mountaineer of all time, Messner, a champion of pared-down 'alpine-style' mountaineering, achieved these momentous feats without the use of supplemental oxygen – something that medical experts once thought was impossible.

Everest Solo Ascent Unpacked

Expedition:
First solo ascent of Everest without supplemental oxygen

Date:
1980

Length:
3 days from base camp

1. Leica camera
2. Trekking trousers
3. Trekking top
4. Crampons
5. Rolex watch
6. Base layer
7. Mittens
8. Fisherman's hat
9. Sailcloth jacket
10. Trekking boots
11. Titanium ice axe
12. Hat
13. Plastic climbing boots
14. Goggles
15. Sunglasses
16. Down sleeping bag
17. Altimeter
18. Expedition suit
19. Gaiters
20. Rucksack
21. Gore-Tex conch tent

EXPEDITIONS UNPACKED

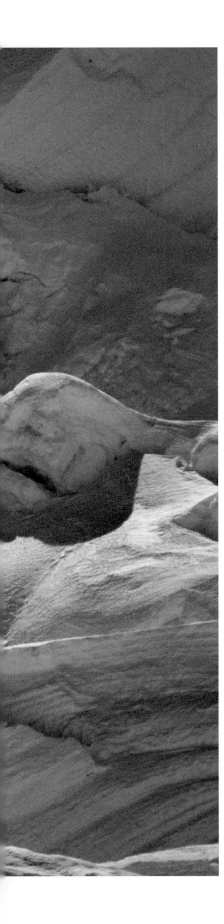

Reinhold Messner considered the 'fast and light' alpine approach to be the purest form of mountaineering. He found the 'siege mentality' employed by large-scale climbing expeditions disrespectful to both nature and the mountains.

His distaste was fuelled by Italian mountaineer Cesare Maestri who, in 1970, dragged a petrol-powered compressor drill up the ice-capped granite needle of Cerro Torre in Southern Patagonia. Driving 400 steel bolts into its sheer southern face, Maestri built a ladder to the top, before abandoning the 90kg (200lb) power tool, leaving it tied to the last anchor bolt, where it still hangs to this day.

In a scathing essay entitled *The Murder of the Impossible*, Messner attacked Maestri's 'conquest alpinism'. From here on, it became Messner's mantra that he would only ascend the world's highest peaks 'by fair means' or not at all.

In 1970, Messner attempted his first major Himalayan climb with his brother, Günther, across the Rupal face of Nanga Parbat. Both men reached the 8,125m (26,657ft) summit, but then the weather deteriorated, forcing them to shelter on the mountain without tents, oxygen or modern down jackets.

Six days later, a dehydrated, frostbitten and delirious Messner stumbled into the valley, but his brother was lost to the mountain, swept off the slopes during the descent by an avalanche.

'When I lost seven of my toes on Nanga Parbat and small parts of my fingertips I knew I'd never be a great rock climber,' Messner has said. 'So I specialised in high-altitude climbing. It's a totally different game. I developed a 15-year passion for it and became maybe even a little narrow-minded in my desire for 8,000-metre peaks.'

Between 1972 and 1986 Messner climbed all the remaining 'eight-thousanders'. In 1978 he climbed Mount Everest, without oxygen, with his Austrian partner, Peter Habeler, supported by a team of nine climbers and several Sherpas. But for the next two years Messner became 'pregnant with this fantasy of soloing Everest'.

Without major financial backers, the 80,000 Deutschmark (£36,000 in 1980; roughly £150,000 today) expedition was largely self-funded. Messner even sold off his prized Porsche 911 just the week before he and his then-girlfriend, Nena Holguin, left for Tibet.

Arriving in the capital, Lhasa, in June 1980, Messner secured the services of a Chinese liaison officer and porter, and two drivers for the decrepit lorry and Jeep that would take them to 5,100m (16,730ft) at the foot of the Rongbuk Valley. Loaded on the back of the truck, the team's gear took up just a quarter of the flatbed – stark contrast to the British-led team for which Edmund Hillary first conquered Everest in 1953, which had engaged twenty Sherpa mountain guides and 350 Nepalese porters to carry 4,536kg (10,000lb) of equipment and provisions to base camp.

But while Hillary had approached from Nepal in the south, Messner would be following the route used by the earlier, ill-fated 1924 British Mount Everest Expedition of George Mallory and Andrew Irvine, which approached from Chinese-controlled Tibet in the north.

While their Chinese assistants used a traditional Yaks wool tent, Messner's were constructed of a waterproof and breathable Gore-Tex material. Just two weeks before leaving on his 1978 expedition to Everest, Messner had watched an impromptu demonstration in the back of a Munich sports shop where a sample of this revolutionary new fabric was stretched over a pot of boiling water; and while the steam came through the membrane, when the pot was turned over, no water seeped back out. Messner was impressed and requested a custom-made Gore-Tex conch tent, the first of its type, which he used at the advanced camps with Habeler.

Now began the process of setting up an intermediate camp at 6,000m (19,685ft), and an advanced camp at 6,500m (21,325ft) from where Messner would strike for the summit when conditions were right. This was the unpredictable monsoon season and he would need a four-day break in the weather to solo to the top. While Holguin prepared food in aluminium pots on the small gas stove, Messner would often climb alone to lay out equipment and supplies in two Gore-Tex tents at the higher camps, slowly acclimatising to the rarefied air, before returning to base to recover.

In partnership with his German sponsors, Adidas, Messner helped develop a new type of lightweight studded trekking shoe, combining the comfort and agility of a running shoe with the ruggedness of a traditional walking boot. Carrying a rucksack weighing just 18kg (40lb) and wearing his lightweight Fila trekking top and trousers, he was able to climb quickly at around 200 vertical metres per hour (650ft), compared to the 25-30m (80-100ft) Hillary's team were averaging at this stage with packs weighing up to 50kg (100lb) per man. Everything Messner carried was pared down to an absolute minimum: 'To be sure, I have only a fraction of what the English lugged up; my climbing aids are light, tested a hundredfold, the best of the best.'

On 17 August 1980 after seven weeks' acclimatisation, both Messner and Holguin, also an accomplished mountaineer, made their way up to 6,500m (21,325ft) for final preparations for the summit offensive.

To conserve time and energy for the final big push, Messner deposited an 'assault pack' 500m (1,640ft) above advanced camp in a hollow below the North Col, containing his down sleeping bag, foam-rubber sleeping mat and a week's supply of food and fuel.

Below Messner and Habeler pose for their sponsors wearing matching Rolex watches and climbing gear supplied by the Italian sportwear manufacturer Fila.

Above Messner and members of the 1978 Austrian expedition to Mount Everest hike across the Western Cwm.

Just before dawn on 18 August 1980, the skies were clear and conditions looked good. By the light of his headtorch Messner went through the practised drill of putting on his Dachstein mittens and 'three layers of clothing – silk, pile suit and thin down suit'. The managing director of Fila was a passionate mountain climber who was keen to promote the brand and produce an outfit that could withstand the harsh mountain conditions. After extensive research, Fila had created the Sailcloth Jacket which Messner wore on Everest, filled with down insulation, and a side gusset to make climbing easier.

As a keen photographer Messner had frequently removed his sunglasses to take snaps of his team-mate Habeler during the 1978 expedition, which resulted in a severe case of snow blindness during the descent. Keen to avoid that same mistake, Messner kept his dark-lensed Carrera glasses in his jacket pocket, ready for the Himalayan sunrise.

Kissing Holguin goodbye he set out with a light rucksack to collect the assault pack he'd stashed the day before. As the snow deepened, Messner switched to his plastic climbing boots, which he had pioneered on Everest in 1978. With a closed-cell foam liner they stayed drier than the traditional leather boot which, when wet, would freeze solid; before the introduction of plastic double-boots, frostbite had claimed the toes of every other climber that had summited an eight-thousander. As temperatures fell to -15°C (5°F), Messner also switched his trademark fisherman's hat for a red Fila woollen one.

As he approached the steeper ground, Messner shortened the length of his two ski poles, using them as a second pair of feet to keep his balance in the soft snow, when all of a sudden the ground gave way. Tumbling into a deep crevasse, his fall was eventually stopped by a metre-wide (3ft) snow bridge: a black abyss to certain death lay either

REINHOLD MESSNER

side. He had no radio on which to call Holguin – contact with the wider world went against his 'alpine' philosophies. Unable to reach the twelve-pointed titanium crampons in his rucksack, it took a Herculean effort to traverse the crevasse wall and haul his way out.

Above 7,500m (23,000ft), Messner came back into Holguin's view through her camera's telephoto lens; she was blissfully unaware of his terrifying near-death experience just moments before. Leaning on his poles he took fifty paces at a time before resting to catch his breath, creating tracks in the snow like 'a chain of pearls'. Messner used these rest stops to take photographs using his 35mm Leica camera, which was attached to his titanium ice axe with a custom-made bracket that allowed it to double as a camera monopod.

As the gradient increased, his progress dropped to thirty paces: 'Breathing is so strenuous that no power to think remains.' Drops of Japanese medicinal oil soothed his ragged throat, but as he tired and became increasingly oxygen starved he imagined that someone was walking alongside him, and the ghosts of Mallory and Irvine began to play on his mind.

Checking the time on his wristwatch (a gifted Rolex from his 1978 expedition), Messner made his bivouac camp at 3 p.m., stretching his tiny 2kg

(4.5lb) Gore-Tex shelter over its light metal poles, and anchoring it down with his ski sticks and the single rock piton he carried. From within this 1.2m (4ft) by 1.8m (6ft) shelter he began six hours of chores, laboriously melting snow to make 'insipid' bowls of soup (at 7,800m (25,590ft) water boils at just 72°C (162°F)).

All that evening, his oxygen-depleted mind began to wander, subconsciously dividing his rations into two portions and talking in Italian, his second language, to an unseen guest before crashing into a fitful night's sleep.

The next morning, after forcing down a breakfast of crumbled cheese on coarse Tyrolean brown bread, he collapsed the tent and loosely tied it to his rucksack, allowing it to air dry and shed some precious weight.

Trudging through knee-deep drifts, Messner was reduced to just fifteen paces between rest stops. Although the original plan had been to follow the 'English Route' and look out for evidence of Mallory and Irvine's 1924 ascent, Messner took the spontaneous decision to follow the North Flank. At 3 p.m., thoroughly exhausted after a 'pain-filled eternity', Messner studied his pocket altimeter and made his second bivouac camp in the Death Zone at 8,220m (28,940ft). At this altitude, with only

thirty per cent of the oxygen found at sea level, the body's cells begin to die, blood thickens and the heart rate soars – Messner's was well over 100 beats per minute.

At 8 a.m. on 20 August 1980, Messner set out for the summit accompanied only by his titanium ice axe, camera and the voices of his imaginary climbing companions. 'After a dozen paces everything in me screams to stop, sit, breathe … I can scarcely go on. No despair. No happiness. No anxiety.'

By midday, as the weather worsened, Messner was forced to crawl on hands and knees just to keep moving forward, until, at around 3 p.m., through the mist and swirling ice crystals, Messner made out the tip of an aluminium survey tripod, left by the Chinese five years earlier, poking through the snow. 'Like a zombie, obeying some inner command', Messner stumbled those last few paces to grasp it 'like a friend', before collapsing, emotionless, at the 8,848m (29,029ft) high summit.

Since 1953 around 5,000 people have climbed Everest, but Messner is the only person who has done it solo and without supplementary oxygen.

What Messner achieved in August 1980, as the renowned American climber Conrad Anker once said: 'Was like landing on the moon. After that, everything else kind of pales in comparison.'

Jason Lewis

Born: 13 September 1967, UK

After pedalling, Rollerblading, trekking and kayaking for thirteen years, across five continents, two oceans and one sea, Jason Lewis became the first person to circumnavigate the planet by human power alone. Expedition 360 took the former window cleaner a decade longer than he had originally planned, setting out in 1994 from his west London squat with his university pal, Steve Smith, and just £319.20 in his pocket. Recent graduates, both men had become disillusioned with the environmental damage caused by our throwaway society, and hoped that an epic carbon-neutral adventure might help them answer some 'big questions'.

Circumnavigation by Human Power Unpacked

Expedition:
First human-powered circumnavigation of the Earth

Date:
1994–2007

Length:
13 years, 2 months and 24 days

1. Kayak
2. Paddle
3. British Army ration packs
4. Sextant
5. Ale
6. Makeshift sea anchor
7. SPD sandals
8. 'Lolita' the lure
9. Viz comics
10. Walkman
11. Ocean ring
12. Rollerblades
13. Mars bars
14. Laptop
15. Whisky
16. Camping stove
17. Satellite phone
18. Wind generator
19. Solar panels
20. Cabbages
21. Handheld GPS
22. Bicycle
23. Radar Reflectors
24. Moksha

As expeditions go, Jason Lewis and Steve Smith's bid to circumnavigate the globe entirely by human power is one of the more unusual.

The pair set off from 0° longitude at the Greenwich Observatory on 12 July 1994 and headed down to Rye on the English south coast. Here they were reunited with Chris Tipper and Hugo Burnham, two newly qualified shipwrights who had constructed a pedal-powered, two-man vessel for crossing the 'big blue bits'.

Christened *Moksha*, Sanskrit for freedom, the 8m (26ft) boat was built from sustainable timber and driven by a twin-bladed propeller through a bicycle crank bolted to the keel. Worryingly, this was the first vessel the pair had ever built, and the English Channel would be its first major sea trial.

While the boat performed well on its 65km (40 mile) crossing to Boulogne, both men quickly realised that they were in no physical shape for the challenge ahead. In the rush to get things together there had been little time to get fit. Instead they decided to 'wait train', postponing all exercise until they were well under way.

They reached the French coast at dusk, slipping the harbour's crane driver a few francs to take Moksha out of the water for her 2,580km (1,600 mile) overland trip to the Atlantic coast of Portugal.

They continued on hybrid bikes, heavily laden with panniers front and rear. Cycling 240km (150 miles) a day, both men's fitness greatly improved by the time they reached Lagos in September.

In a frenzied four weeks *Moksha* was refitted with radar reflectors, wind generators and solar panels. Inside the cramped cabin, a canvas bed was fitted in a sleeping compartment at the front, christened the 'rat hole'; 'with dimensions comparable to a snug coffin', this was the only place they could fully stretch out and get some much-needed rest between the three-hour pedalling shifts.

Designed to carry enough food and provisions for two people for up to 150 days, everything was weighed on a set of bathroom scales before being stowed, to ensure the cargo was evenly spread. Although they had a 10 litre (2 gallon) canvas water bag onboard, most fresh water would come from the handheld desalinisation pump, which needed to be worked for three hours a day to generate the 12 litres (2.6 gallons) needed to stay hydrated.

The day before they left, Smith underwent a crash course in navigating by sextant from a concerned local yachtsman, who also advised they fit a makeshift sea anchor, made from an old car tyre lashed to a long rope, which would help keep *Moksha* perpendicular to the waves and less likely to capsize.

Nursing savage hangovers from their goodbye party, the two set off in early October 1994. There was no turning back now as the Canary Current pushed them southwest into the Atlantic.

For financial reasons, the plan was to head west towards Florida. Expedition 360 had not managed to attract any financial backers at this stage and it was hoped that American sponsors might come

on board. However, some companies had donated supplies and equipment, including the RAF, who had given two lifejackets, Mars UK had provided 4,000 chocolate bars and the British Army had donated 250 ration packs (only later did they realise that these were six years out of date).

For the first 560km (350 miles), conditions were kind, but on the twelfth day, 4.5m (15ft) rollers battered the boat – its first real test in heavy seas. Over the crackling VHF radio a passing Filipino cargo ship offered to rescue them; its kindly captain taking a while to grasp the mad idea that they were not adrift, but pedalling across the Atlantic. 'Which nationality are you?' he asked. 'English', replied Smith. 'Ah, OK. I am understanding now,' he signed off.

After resting in Madeira, the pair returned to the 'all-consuming state of drudgery … like lobotomized hamsters chained to a wheel', moving at an average speed of just 3km/h (1.5 knots). At the end of each three-hour shift the men unclipped their sandals from the pedals and rewarded themselves with tea and Mars bars; every 480km (300 miles), as they crossed each five-degree line

of longitude, they congratulated themselves with a hearty swig of Ballantine's whisky. Nevertheless, burning 8,000 calories each day the pair looked decidedly gaunt by the time they reached Miami on 17 February 1995, after 111 days at sea.

Thor Heyerdahl had called it 'expedition fever', when extended periods in close proximity to your crewmates start to drive you insane. To give each other a bit of space, Smith crossed the 4,000km (2,500 miles) from Florida to California on bike through the southern states, while Lewis set out to Rollerblade via the American midwest. The only drawback being that he had never Rollerbladed before in his life.

Managing just 1.6km (1 mile) on his first day, it was a steep learning curve for Lewis, but he was strong and enjoying the freedom of travelling alone on his Rollerblades. Reaching the halfway point near Pueblo, Colorado, Lewis was coming to the end of a mammoth 112km (70 mile) day when, out of nowhere, a drunk driver travelling at 65km/h (40mph) hit him from behind. As he later wrote: 'I tried to stand up, but something wasn't right … Instead of feet, I was standing on the stumps of my

JASON LEWIS

EXPEDITIONS UNPACKED

lower legs, tibias jammed in the dirt.' The 82-year-old driver later told police that he thought he'd hit a deer – a strange excuse considering Lewis's rucksack had gone through his windshield.

Nine months later, with titanium rods pinning his shattered bones together, Lewis picked up his route again, from the exact same spot in Pueblo. He completed the remaining 1,200km (750 miles) to San Francisco, to become the first person ever to Rollerblade across the USA.

In California, he met back up with his shipmate Smith, and they pedalled *Moksha* together for the first leg over the Pacific. But, in February 1999, after completing the 54-day crossing to Hawaii, Smith decided to leave Expedition 360. However, before the two men parted company they mustered a group of adventurous souls to join them on a four-day, 130km (80 mile) hike across the island, climbing the 2,000m (6,500ft) pass between the volcanoes of Mauna Loa and Mauna Kea, through dramatic lava fields towards Kona.

Back aboard *Moksha*, Lewis spent the next 73 days alone, pedalling for 15 hours a day against strong counter currents, only to find in the morning, when he switched on his handheld GPS, that he'd been dragged back to where he started. Mentally, these were tough times, made worse by the large boils (known as salt sores) erupting over his body. Only a quick diagnosis by a dermatologist over the satellite phone, and a dose of broad-spectrum antibiotics, prevented blood poisoning spreading to his brain with fatal consequences.

To stave off scurvy Lewis had brought five cabbages on board, eating one leaf a day to get his Vitamin C fix. As he headed out into the warmer waters of the South Pacific the fish were plentiful and easily caught with 'Lolita' the lure. Gutted on the wooden breadboard/chart table, these were fried on the small camping stove, which hung from a rack made from a repurposed bike pannier.

Lewis had only a curious white-tip shark for company during this lonely 4,350km (2,700 mile) crossing to Tarawa in the middle of the Pacific Ocean. He had, however, more than ninety letters from family and friends aboard, which he would open at particularly low moments; emails were always welcome, picked up on his ruggedised PC laptop. Other home comforts included a shortwave radio, a Walkman cassette player for pedalling motivation and twenty *Viz* comics: 'Forget anything more intellectually demanding. Your head is boiled after a month of sleep deprivation,' he wrote in his blog. There was also a jar of Marmite aboard; this sticky brown spread, and much-loved British delicacy, helped with seasickness and was a taste of home; but it was also Lewis's backup plan if he were to encounter pirates on the high seas: 'You smear it on yourself and pretend you've gone all Mr Kurtz, using your own excrement as sunscreen. They won't come near you.'

Genuinely fearing for his sanity during that long Pacific voyage Lewis invited others to join him at every opportunity, starting with Tipper the boatbuilder for the 2,000km (1,300 mile) pedal to the Solomon Islands. When they arrived in June 2000 a bloody feud was raging between the islanders of Malaita and Guadalcanal. Most foreigners had already been evacuated and the *Moksha* had to reroute through the Mboli Passage: a treacherous channel inhabited by a large population of saltwater crocodile.

The Coral Sea, off the northeast coast of Australia, has a fearsome reputation and 50km/h (25 knot) southeasterlies threatened to dash the boat on the Great Barrier Reef. Struggling to find a way through, Lewis transferred to a kayak for the 35km (22 mile) paddle to the shores of northern Queensland. Before he reached the nearest settlement, a 4.5m (15ft) crocodile took an interest in the canoe, mistaking it for a young male croc encroaching on his territory. Lewis fended it off by thrusting his wooden paddle down its throat.

In Australia, Lewis set off on an 88-day outback odyssey on mountain bikes loaned by Cannondale,

with a group of environmentally minded students and educators, towards Alice Springs and then north to Darwin.

After a three-year hiatus in the expedition, while Lewis raised more funds, he was reunited with *Moksha* in May 2005 to cross the Timor Sea. For the next two years, he would kayak and cycle his way up through Indonesia, Singapore, Thailand and Laos towards China, trekking over the Tibetan Plateau and the foothills of the Himalayas. He mountain biked 1,600km (1,000 miles) through eastern Tibet, mostly at night to avoid the Chinese police checkpoints, then turned south, across Nepal and towards the Indian port of Mumbai.

With help from the Royal Bombay Yacht Club, *Moksha* was made shipshape for her voyage across the Arabian Sea to Djibouti on the African coast.

Travelling up through East Africa and into Jordan, Syria and Turkey, Lewis then cycled across Europe to the French port of Cap Gris-Nez in just eight weeks. Slipping on his silver 'ocean ring' (a good luck charm he'd worn for every sea crossing) for one last time, he boarded *Moksha* for the final pedal across the Channel, after spending almost a third of his lifetime travelling 74,843km (46,505 miles) around the globe by human power alone.

Expedition 360 wasn't just about breaking records; Lewis had promoted environmental responsibility and global citizenship around the world, and proved that it is possible to achieve amazing feats without fossil fuels.

In Lewis's quest to answer some 'big questions', Expedition 360 had been a test of both physical endurance and mental strength. 'The human body is capable of incredible feats of endurance – but only if the mind buys into it.' He demonstrated, that if you remain persistent, use imagination and stay focused, nothing is impossible.

Below Lewis returns to the River Thames after more than 13 years and 74,843km (46,505 miles) on Expedition 360's human-powered circumnavigation of the globe.

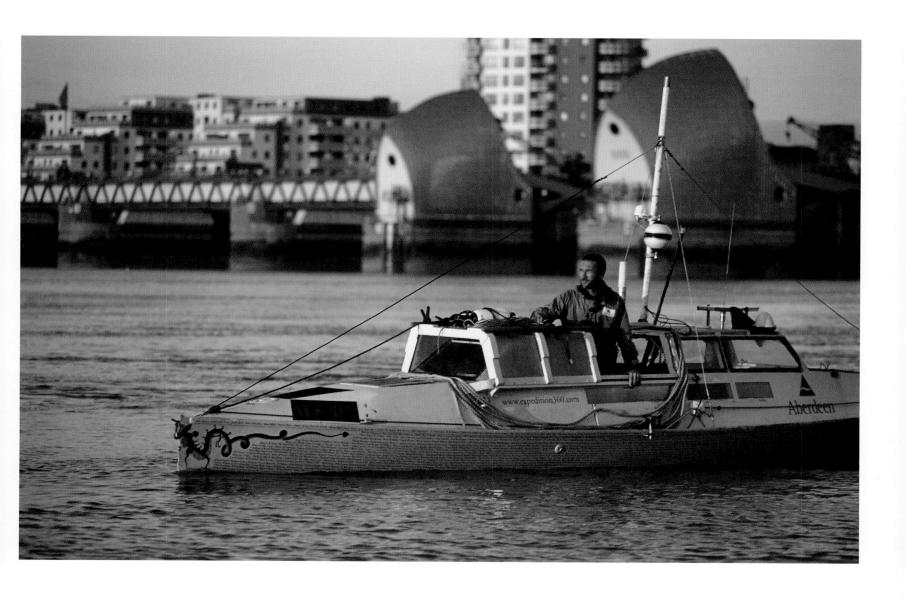

Alastair Humphreys

Born: 27 November 1976, UK

Born in Yorkshire, England, this former National Geographic Explorer of the Year began a four-year challenge in 2001 to cycle around the world. Whenever asked: 'What is the hardest thing you have ever done?' Alastair Humphreys modestly admits it was cycling that first mile, away from everyone he loved, a safe career and a comfortable home, combined with the fear of failure and looking foolish. The Scandinavians call this the 'doorstep mile'. However, Humphreys decided that: 'the only thing worse than making an idiot of myself, would be to grow old, look back, and really regret not having a go.'

Cycle Around the World Unpacked

Expedition:
Cycle around the world

Date:
2001–2005

Length:
4 years 3 months

1. Tent
2. Cycle helmet
3. Cotton T-shirt
4. Water bottle
5. Duct tape
6. Zip-off trousers
7. Sunglasses
8. Zip ties
9. Multi-tool
10. Trainers
11. Long-sleeved shirt
12. Valenkis
13. Baseball cap
14. Mosquito net
15. Hat
16. Sheep fleece gloves
17. Reindeer-fur saddle cover
18. Bungee cords
19. Pierre Jourdan champagne
20. Stove
21. Leatherman penknife
22. Odometer
23. Books
24. Panniers
25. Spare bike chain
26. Spare tyre
27. LED head torch
28. Superglue
29. Bike pump
30. Fingerless cycling gloves
31. Toothbrush and spoon
32. SPD sandals
33. First aid kit
34. Maps
35. Specialized Rockhopper mountain bike

Right Camping on the Uyuni Salt Flats of Bolivia, the dried-up remains of a prehistoric lake. To survive the intense heat, Alastair Humphreys carried 18 litres (4.8 gallons) of drinking water in his panniers.

In a 2013 *TED Talk*, Alastair Humphreys claimed that it is remarkably easy to cycle around the world: 'If you can ride a bike for a day and put up a tent, then you have all the skills and equipment necessary…' as long as you have the willpower to keep going.

That was all it took for Humphreys to begin his pedal-powered circumnavigation of the globe in August 2001. He set off from his parents' home in Airton, Yorkshire, with his mother's tinfoil-wrapped sandwiches tucked in his pocket, and his father redirecting him back onto the right road out of the village.

Before the journey he had never spent a night alone in a tent, but now he would have to wild camp wherever he could, in an attempt to keep costs down. It was unnerving at first, but his freestanding Coleman tent was small enough to go undetected in patches of woodland or hidden fields, and he began to relish the 'nights of free freedom in fun and beautiful spots' as he pedalled through rural Belgium and France. Surviving on a budget of less than £5 per day, and in an effort to minimise weight, Humphreys picked up fresh local produce in the markets he passed through, all cooked up on his multi-fuel MSR Whisperlite stove, which could run on anything from petrol to Russian vodka.

With £7,000 saved from his student loan to fund the entire expedition, Alastair set out on a steel-framed Specialized Rockhopper mountain bike, which was slowly upgraded with a more comfortable saddle, stronger rims and tyres as the journey progressed. The four panniers fitted front and rear had dry bags inside to make them fully waterproof. Equipped with a basic grasp of bike maintenance, he carried a spare tyre across the back rack, and in the bottom of one pannier a set of spare brake blocks, pump, a replacement chain (switched every 3,000km/1,860 miles) and spokes; as well as other stuff he hoped not to use too often, including a first aid kit and the greatest repair tools known to mankind: duct tape, superglue and zip ties.

The front right pannier, the most accessible of the four, was where the maps, diary, Olympus compact camera and his favourite paperbacks were kept. Despite every effort to travel light (in these days before the e-reader), books took up an enormous amount of space, sometimes carrying up to a dozen onboard at a time. These initially included the *SAS Survival Handbook* – 'with manly plans that never materialized of catching my own food and navigating by the stars' – the latest *Harry Potter* and a brick-like *History of the World*, which he admitted: 'Was a little excessive, perhaps, especially considering that I had not packed any underwear to save some weight.'

'There are six things you dream of on a cycling holiday: flat, smooth tarmac, beautiful scenery, easy navigation, delicious food, a welcoming bed and an enticing final destination. The Danube River has it all,' he wrote. By late September, as his fitness improved, Humphreys was enjoying 100km (60 mile) days in the saddle, stopping at hospitable Austrian campsites. By the middle of October he had crossed his first continent and was cycling through the sprawling metropolis of Istanbul: 'I find stalls packed tight together, humanity filling the gaps and huge barrows of hazelnuts or pistachio nuts manoeuvring impossibly through it all.' At this stage Turkey, with its markets and minarets, felt strange and exotic – returning back this way four years later it would seem like he was almost home.

From Turkey, the original plan was to continue heading east. Humphrey's passport already bore visa stamps for Iran and Pakistan, and cold-weather gear including down-filled jackets and sleeping bags were packed in the panniers. But the political shockwaves of the 9/11 attacks in the USA now made that route across Asia a less attractive prospect. Weighing up all options Humphreys decided to head south, towards Africa.

On 24 November 2001, he reached Lebanon: 'A tiny nation combining natural beauty with some of the juiciest history in the world. The best food in the Middle East, and a buzzing, invigorated capital city.' As the temperatures rose, Humphreys switched to sandals, which clipped into his bike pedals, and put on his baseball cap, sunscreen and his prized Oakley sunglasses. Staying hydrated now became a growing concern, filling the 10-litre (2-gallon) water bag whenever possible to increase his cycling range.

After passing the sun-parched shores of Jordan's Dead Sea, Christmas Day 2001 was spent riding

Below Humphreys kept a photo diary of his travels around the globe, mastering the art of the well-framed selfie with his compact digital camera.

the biblical King's Highway towards the 'lost' kingdom of Petra, stopping only for a festive breakfast of deep-fried falafel and hot sweet tea. The endless mountain roads, rough camping and basic food was beginning to take its toll, and a much-needed rest at Aqaba on the Red Sea marked the end of another continent. Egypt, and the beginning of Humphreys' African odyssey was now just a short ferry trip away.

Escaping the mayhem and tacky tourist developments of Cairo, Humphreys was glad to head south, along the lush Nile valley, towards the shores of Lake Nasser from where he'd take the daily 24-hour ferry to Sudan. On disembarking he found that disentangling *Rita*, Alastair's faithfull Specialized mountain bike, from the sea of humanity crammed below decks was no easy feat: 'Heavy sacks were dumped on top of boxes of soft fruit, rainbows of stacked plastic chairs jumbled amongst bags of already spilling sugar.'

After docking – and paying mysterious fees, signing passports and collecting stamps – Humphreys headed out of Wadi Halfa on the corrugated road of gravel and dust with his face wrapped up in a sandstorm face mask.

For two weeks he pushed and pedalled in stifling 45°C (113°F) heat; permanently encrusted with sweat and grime, his ragged, salt-stained zip-off trousers and cotton T-shirts were now held together with safety pins and duct tape. As the oppressive temperatures subsided each evening, Humphreys made camp, laying out his inflatable mattress and sleeping bag beneath a mosquito net draped over his bike frame.

One night, camping on a wide scenic bend of the Nile, the desire to wash and cool off nearly overrode his instinctive fear of crocodiles. Only when he returned later that evening with his LED headtorch to see golf ball-sized eyes peaking out of the water, did he realise his instincts had been right.

Weighing almost 60kg (130lb), the overloaded bike's frame finally snapped on a punishing stretch of rutted road. In the next village a local welder made temporary repairs as best he could, refusing payment and loading Humphreys' panniers with cookies for the road. He was utterly humbled by the kindness of the people he met in Sudan, spending several happy weeks in Khartoum teaching English, PE and attempting to introduce schoolchildren to the joys of cricket.

Below Humphreys' circumnavigation was described by Sir Ranulph Fiennes as 'the first great adventure of the millennium ... an old-fashioned expedition: long, lonely, low-budget and spontaneous.'

EXPEDITIONS UNPACKED

Left Navigating the featureless deserts of Sudan with a 1:500,000 scale road map was no easy task.

Collecting a replacement Rockhopper in Ethiopia, he began the long ride down the east coast of Africa through Kenya, the tea plantations of Tanzania, along the shores of Lake Malawi and Zimbabwe. Reaching South Africa in late September 2002, Humphreys took on the Sani Pass, climbing 1,332m (4,370ft) up 1:3 gravel roads to Lesotho via a series of terrifying hairpin bends.

After the rigours of Africa's gravel roads, *Rita II* was now in pretty bad shape: a cracked pannier was lashed together with a spoon and string, broken gears had to be changed by moving the chain with an old toothbrush, and a scrap of wellington boot plugged a hole in his worn-out tyre. Nevertheless, on 20 October 2002, after 422 days, 20,300km (12,600 miles) and 27 countries, Humphreys reached Cape Town on the southern tip of Africa. 'Having omitted to pack a cavalry sabre in my panniers I had to resort to scything open my Pierre Jourdan champagne with my Leatherman penknife. A crisp "pop" and time to celebrate.'

Working his passage across the Atlantic, aboard the 18m (58ft) yacht *Maiden*, Humphreys enjoyed the varied company of his fifteen crewmates during the 24-day crossing, arriving in Rio de Janeiro at the dead of night, beneath the illuminated statue of Christ the Redeemer in February 2003. However, Humphreys was determined to cycle the length of the Americas, from Argentina to Alaska, which required an uncomfortable five-day bus ride south.

From Patagonia he: 'rode through temperate dripping forests, tatty and lichen covered, deep and mysterious like *The Lord of the Rings*'. Beyond the mountains of Tierra del Fuego he arrived at the flat soggy moorland of the pampa with ferocious biting winds – for two days he had to push the bike, huddling under bushes at night when he could no longer stand up.

Chile's Carretera Austral was the scenic highlight of Humphreys' adventure, running for 1,240 breath-taking kilometres (770 miles) through dense forest, snow-capped volcanoes and glacial streams teeming with trout. In theory, navigation through the Americas should have been a doddle, with the Pan-America Highway linking the entirety of South, Central, and North America. The only snag was the 160km (100 mile) Darién Gap in northern Colombia, an impenetrable mix of

Below Silhoutted against the sunset, Humphreys is photographed on Turkey's Black Sea coast after four years on the road.

EXPEDITIONS UNPACKED

Left *Rita*, Humphreys' faithful Specialized mountain bike, crossed every extreme, from the red sand deserts of Jordan to the icy wastelands of Siberia, during his four-year adventure.

tropical forest and swampland that was home to deadly snakes, poisonous spiders, gun-toting drug smugglers and Cuban-backed guerrillas.

Humphreys worked his way around this problem by crewing on the pleasure yacht *Hannah Rose* with his sorry-looking, salt-encrusted and rust-streaked bike lashed to the stern railings.

By the time Humphreys reached Arizona, *Rita II* had completely given up the ghost; only a generous whip-round from various Mormon and Baptist churches got him back on the road with a sturdy steel-framed mountain bike.

From Alaska, Humphreys made his way over to Russia by freighter, cycling the infamous 'Road of Bones' through Siberia where the -45°C (-49°F) cracked the plastic windows of his tent. He bought extra foam sleeping mats, sheep fleece gloves and the local *valenkis* (a kind of carpeted boot) from hunting stores in a desperate bid to keep warm. One generous Russian made him a reindeer-fur saddle cover to stop his bum from freezing to the bike.

To smooth over any run-ins with police or officious bureaucrats, Humphreys carried his 'Magic Letter', an introduction and explanation of what he was trying to achieve, translated into the language of every region he planned to pass through. In China this was supplemented with a series of flash cards bearing helpful phrases such as: 'I want to eat something large and cheap', which invariably produced heaps of steaming noodles.

After months of cycling through the Russian-speaking 'Stans', in August 2005 Humphreys crossed the Bosphorus, back into Europe and, after a couple of months more, to the Yorkshire Dales. A journey of 74,000km (46,000 miles), through 60 countries and five continents, had taken Humphreys four and a quarter years to complete.

Sir Ranulph Fiennes later wrote that Humphreys' trip: 'was probably the first great adventure of the millennium … an old-fashioned expedition: long, lonely, low-budget and spontaneous.'

In his typical self-deprecating style, Humphreys believes that if he can cycle around the world, then pretty much anyone can: 'I am not a cyclist. I'm not very brave. I didn't have much cash. I didn't have the best gear.' Of all the important lessons he learned about himself during his many years on the road, at the top of his list was the belief that: 'You are capable of more than you realize. The doorstep mile – the very first one – is the hardest of all.'

ALASTAIR HUMPHREYS

Rune Gjeldnes

Born: 20 May 1971, Norway

In 2006, former Norwegian Navy commando, Rune Gjeldnes, became the first man to traverse the planet's three largest ice caps, across the Arctic, Greenland and Antarctica, a feat known as the 'triple crown' of polar exploration. The final part of this achievement he called 'The Longest March' – a solo kite-ski trek from the Russian research base at Queen Maud Land, over the South Pole to Terra Nova Bay without support or resupply. This distance of 4,804km (2,985 miles) smashed the previous ski-journey distance record by more than 1,000km (620 miles).

The Longest March Unpacked

Expedition:
Longest solo ski journey

Date:
2005 to 2006

Length:
90 days

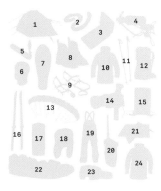

1. Tent
2. Golden tinsel
3. Magnetic compass
4. Multi-fuel stove
5. Cigar
6. Neoprene face mask
7. Down-filled sleeping bag
8. Ski boots
9. Aluminium crampons
10. Down parka
11. Ski poles
12. Rucksack
13. Kite

14. Camera
15. iPod
16. Walking skis
17. Iridium satellite phone
18. Hat
19. Salopettes
20. Electronic beacon
21. Maps
22. Pulk
23. Ski goggles
24. Jacket

Although Rune Gjeldnes had already been to the North Pole, much of the equipment used for his Longest March expedition had to be redesigned for use in Antarctica, including his 2.5m (8ft) pulk – a type of low-slung toboggan constructed of lightweight Kevlar and carbon fibre. While the Norwegian firm Acapulka had previously supplied Gjeldnes with shorter pulks capable of floating across Arctic ice floes, the priority for the South Pole would be lightness, a tough underbody construction to cope with the never-ending sastrugi (wave-like ridges of hard snow resembling sand dunes) and exceptional stability when anchored to the sail kites. Weighing just 12kg (26lb) when fully fitted out, the Trans Antarctic Challenge 250 model could also double as an emergency bivouac when winds got too high to erect the tent.

Heading out from the Russian research base on 6 November 2005, the initial climb was much steeper than Gjeldnes had anticipated, and with a strong headwind it was not possible to get the sail kites airborne. Heavily laden with 180kg (400lb) worth of provisions and equipment, Gjeldnes instead had to use his walking skis fitted with short skins for the long climb up to the Antarctic Plateau. Traditionally made of sealskin, modern-day nylon versions of skins attach to the skis with a loop over the tip and adhesive on the base, and allow the ski to slide forward but not backwards. Leaning on his aluminium ski poles, Gjeldnes managed just 5km (3 miles) on that first gruelling day.

On his back Gjeldnes carried a 20kg (44lb) rucksack containing emergency supplies, spare woollen mittens, clothing and backup communication equipment. The rucksack was supplied by Bergans of Norway, the renowned outdoor equipment company that patented the rucksack, as we know it, and equipped many expeditions in the heroic age of polar exploration, including Amundsen and Scott during their race to the South Pole.

After four days the weather broke and Gjeldnes was able to launch a kite. At the end of a 60m (200ft) line, the large parafoil (similar to that used by kite surfers) increased Gjeldnes' distances to more than 65km (40 miles) a day on this tough climb up the fractured glacier towards the plateau. Gjeldnes carried kites of different sizes to suit different weather conditions; when winds were very low he would have to run with it behind him to get it airborne and high enough to find stronger winds – it was exhausting work, running in cumbersome ski boots through 40cm (15in) of snow, wrapped up in layers of thick polar clothing.

At the end of each eight-hour stint Gjeldnes would erect his custom-designed two-man tent. Several prototypes had been made and cold-weather tested by his equipment sponsors. The final version of Bergans' Antarctica tent featured a single breathable outer layer with a second inner tent to provide insulation against the -50°C (-58°F) night time temperatures. Weighing just 3kg (7lb), it was designed to be put up quickly by just one man (Gjeldnes practised hard to get that down to less than four minutes) and have extremely low wind resistance.

The first real test came after a week on the ice when Gjeldnes' pulk slid into a hidden

RUNE GJELDNES

EXPEDITIONS UNPACKED

crevasse. Still heavily laden at this early stage of the expedition, it nearly dragged him down, too; only a swift manoeuvre to anchor himself with his skis averted disaster. Over the next few days the crevasses grew bigger and Gjeldnes had to ski over narrow snow bridges wherever he could. A few days of heavy snow not only made spotting them harder, it also increased the friction between the surface and the pulk's polyethylene-coated runners. It was hot, sweaty work, and Gjeldnes was sometimes forced to strip to just his underwear beneath his thick down-filled Bergans parka and salopettes to regulate his core temperature and maintain optimum performance. Unlike his fellow countryman, Roald Amundsen, from a century earlier, Gjeldnes' expedition had an important scientific element; regular blood samples were taken to be used in studies by the US and Norwegian Navy on how the human immune system responded in extreme conditions.

By 17 November 2005, the treacherous glaciers and crevasses were behind him. Stronger winds, and level ground at 3,000m (9,800ft) above sea level on the Antarctic Plateau, meant Gjeldnes could fully exploit his kite's towing power, covering 100km (60 miles) on a good day. However, as the temperatures began to drop, Gjeldnes became increasingly worried about frostbite in his feet. Clipped into bindings on his longer sledging skis, he couldn't move his toes much to generate heat or keep the circulation moving. But he did his best to keep these extremities warm and dry with gaiters keeping out the snow, moisture-block socks and woollen inner shoes inside his ski boots.

When the winds disappeared Gjeldnes made the best of the rest days repairing equipment and adding extra insulation to his ski boots. He also updated his daily journals and uploaded expedition photographs via his Motorola Iridium satellite phone. The enforced rest stops were also a good opportunity for Gjeldnes to take on some extra calories and fluid; on the toughest days he could be burning up to 9,000

and needed to hydrate regularly in the dry polar air. Early each evening he cooked up 1kg (2.2lb) of dehydrated food in lightweight pans on his multi-fuel stove; this soon became the highlight of the day, along with the warmth and comfort of his down-filled sleeping bag and Therma-a-Rest sleeping mattress. The only real luxury Gjeldnes carried in his 'fun bag', along with his diary, pictures from home and toothbrush, was an iPod loaded with 500 tunes. To escape the boredom and loneliness, Gjeldnes also sent daily dispatches and sketches from his satellite phone about the farm that he hoped to buy with his girlfriend, Aina, when he returned home from Antarctica.

Over the next two weeks the sastrugi became an increasing hazard, now approaching 2m (7ft) in height, and Gjeldnes had to concentrate hard to avoid catching his ski tips and flipping over the pulk. When he finally reached the Geographical South Pole on 20 December 2005 at 12.46 p.m. Greenwich Mean Time, he had been skiing for 45 days and had covered 2,200km (1,370 miles) alone and without resupplies. Exhausted, physically and mentally, he made camp that night in an area crisscrossed with Caterpillar tracks leading to the American Amundsen-Scott base, only to be woken a few hours later by the roar of a four-engined Hercules transport aircraft coming into land just 50m (160ft) above his tent.

Turbulent winds began to slow his daily progress to just 25km (15 miles) a day, before the winds dropped completely and it began to snow. Christmas Day 2005 was a complete whiteout and Gjeldnes used it as a great excuse to decorate the tent with some golden tinsel, and relax with Bing Crosby's *White Christmas* on his iPod while enjoying a celebratory cigar and the dried meat Aina had wrapped as a Christmas present.

By the New Year, Gjeldnes had entered a region of more stable winds and was now making around 150km (90 miles) each day, only slowing down

Opposite top Gjeldnes rests on his pulk to take on water and stave of dehydration in the dry polar air. In the background low-lying sastrugi (wave-like ice formations) are starting to form.

Opposite bottom Weighing just 3kg (6lb 10oz), Gjeldnes' custom-made 'Antarctica' tent provided excellent insulation against the night-time temperatures, which dropped to around -50°C (-58°F).

to repair broken kite lines and to dance about the ice in a desperate attempt to get some heat into his bitterly cold feet, which were now showing the early signs of frostbite. Although it was bright and sunny, Gjeldnes had to cover his face with a black neoprene Gator mask to keep out the biting polar winds and iridescent-lensed ski goggles to protect his eyes from harmful UV rays.

On 3 January 2006, Gjeldnes' GPS tracker showed that he had skied more than 2,845km (1,768 miles), beating the solo ski trek record. After six more days, he broke the record for the furthest ever unsupported ski journey, too (previously held by two Norwegians, Eirik Sønneland and Rolf Bae). He had taken 68 days to cover 3,880km (2,411 miles).

To keep supporters back home updated of his progress, Gjeldnes carried an Argos transmitter that sent an update of his location, ground temperature and altitude every hour. In case of emergency he also carried the type of electronic beacon that had been designed as a location device primarily to locate downed military aircraft. However, day-to-day navigation was achieved with a far more basic magnetic compass and paper maps.

Conditions remained perfect over the next week, with stiff winds on day 72 helping Gjeldnes set a new personal best of 211km (131 miles) in a single day as he sped towards the Trans Antarctic Mountains. With the smell of the ocean beginning to fill his nostrils, he pushed hard, kiting at 25-30km/h (15-18mph) through some of the worst sastrugi encountered so far.

After a two-day white-out spent resting in his tent, Gjeldnes re-emerged to start making preparations for the descent of the crevasse-strewn Priestly Glacier, only to discover that one of his walking skis had been thrown from the sledge as it had bucked over the sastrugi. Much of the final leg would now have to be completed on foot wearing his aluminium crampons to gain purchase on the hard blue ice, utilising ice bolts and 30m (100ft) of climbing rope

to traverse the most treacherous sections.

By 24 January 2006, 'Rune was literally walking on the edge', reported his support team. Just four days later, the last Russian Ilyushin aircraft flew out of the airstrip at Patriot Hills Base Camp bound for Punta Arenas, Chile, marking the end of the Antarctic expedition season. Gjeldnes was now one of the last men left on the ice as progress slowed to barely 10km (6 miles) per day on the perilous descent towards the Italian research base at Terra Nova Bay. Stopping to photograph a particularly hazardous crevasse field that Gjeldnes had nicknamed 'The Road From Hell', he stumbled and dropped his compact camera into a gaping abyss. Fatigue was now clearly taking its toll.

However, as Gjeldnes later wrote: 'The body can do a lot if the mind will let it.' With only 40km (25 miles) and one mountain ridge remaining, it took Gjeldnes two days of single-minded determination to cross the steep and slippery path across the northern foothills before the Southern Ocean came into view.

On 3 February 2006, the message was transmitted: 'It's a new page in Polar History: Norwegian Rune Gjeldnes has reached Terra Nova Base today at 2:00 CET. The longest Antarctic polar march ever without resupplies!' Gjeldnes had finally completed The Longest March, a 4,804km (2,985 mile) unsupported kite trek across Antarctica; the equivalent of going from Los Angeles to New York plus a further 322km (200 miles). Not only had Gjeldnes beaten the previous record by more than 1,000km (620 miles), he had also beaten his own agenda, completing the crossing in just 90 days, 20 days quicker than he had originally planned.

In 2012, Gjeldnes was awarded the Mungo Park Medal by the Royal Scottish Geographical Society in recognition of his outstanding contribution to geographical science through exploration – the second Norwegian to ever be awarded this prestigious medal, since Thor Heyerdahl in 1950 for the Kon-Tiki expedition in the South Pacific.

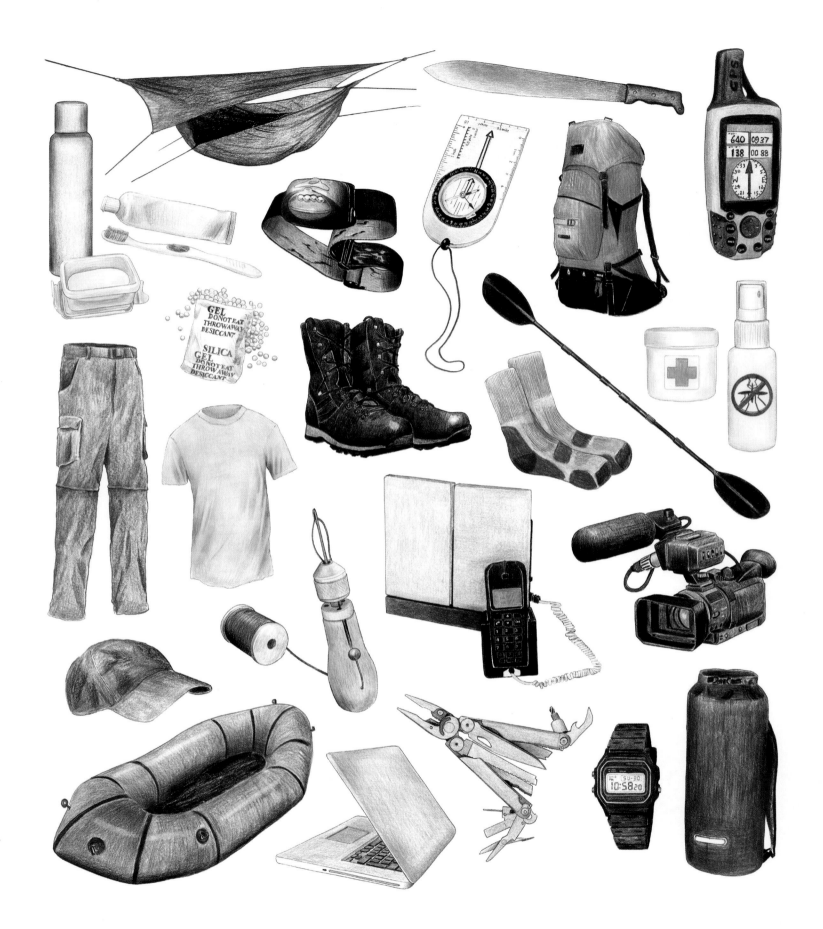

Ed Stafford

Born: 26 December 1975, UK

As a restless schoolboy I was always fascinated by the tales of the great polar explorers. My childhood heroes were globetrotters, solo yachtsmen, Everest summiteers and legendary adventurers such as Sir Ranulph Fiennes. I travelled the world as a Captain in the British Army, but by my early thirties I had become obsessed with the idea of 'doing something amazing'. And so, on 1 April 2008, I found myself on a Peruvian beach, ankle-deep in the Pacific Ocean, ready to make the first of nine million steps that would take me across South America to become the first man to walk the course of the Amazon, from its source in the Andes to the shores of the Atlantic.

Walking the Amazon Unpacked

Expedition:
Walking the Amazon

Date:
2008–2010

Length:
860 days

1.	Hammock and flysheet	14.	Carbon-fibre paddles
2.	Machete	15.	Petroleum jelly
3.	Wash kit	16.	DEET 50%
4.	Toothpaste and toothbrush	17.	Peaked baseball cap
5.	Head torch	18.	Speedy Stitcher sewing awl
6.	Compass	19.	Satellite communication equipment
7.	Rucksack		
8.	Global positioning system	20.	Camcorder
9.	Silica gel sachets	21.	Packraft
10.	Loose-fitting trekking trousers	22.	Laptop
11.	T-shirt	23.	Leatherman multitool
12.	Boots	24.	Watch
13.	Trekking socks	25	Waterproof dry bag

EXPEDITIONS UNPACKED

Setting out with Luke Collyer, an expedition leader I had worked with in Belize, it took us twenty-four days to reach the summit of Nevado Mismi at 5,597m (18,363ft), the official source of the Amazon, from where a trickle of meltwater splashed eastwards into the Carhuasanta Valley below. Walking downhill, through the barren treeless landscape, alongside the tiny snaking stream, it was easy navigation at this stage: we had good 1:100,000 military-grade topographic maps and a state-of-the-art Garmin GPS unit that could be pre-programmed with coordinates and featured an electronic compass and altimeter.

The reception we received at these mountain villages varied from open-armed welcomes to outright hostility. Some Peruvians in these parts were suspicious of the 'gringos' – they believed that white men hunted indigenous people to harvest their organs. Others believed that we were here to steal their children and their lands, and would often reach for shotguns and bows as we approached. To try and ingratiate ourselves with the locals, we often carried extra items of fishing tackle – hooks, weights and nylon line – to offer as gifts, just as Lieutenant Colonel Percy Fawcett had done a century earlier.

Reaching the city of Cusco on 26 May 2008, we ditched as much of our cold-weather gear as we could; jackets, thermals, waterproofs and our thick goose-down sleeping bags were all sent back to England. My 90 litre (20 gallon) rucksack was now down to a more sensible 32kg (70lb) – without food – and was no longer, quite literally, bursting at the seams, having been repaired several times using my Speedy Stitcher sewing awl.

In mid-July we reached the Apurimac, the deepest canyon on the planet, and the beginning of Peru's notorious Red Zone; a lawless region controlled by cocaine traffickers and dotted with coca-processing plants. It was here that Collyer decided to leave the expedition – our relationship had become strained and I was glad to have the freedom to do things my way. From this point on I relied on local guides – both for their diplomatic skills with neighbouring villages, and their knowledge of the local geography.

I was now entering the Amazon rainforest just as I had imagined it from my geography lessons at school: a dark, humid, wall of vegetation; full of exotic wildlife and the booming sound of howler monkeys high in the jungle canopy. Hacking a path through the overgrown eastern valley, away from the drug lords on the western bank, was slow, back-breaking work. Getting adequate rest at the end of a long day became vitally important, and

having ditched the tents, we were now sleeping in parachute silk hammocks strung between the trees. These were fitted with a bespoke 'Guyana-style' mosquito nets, which were 100% insect proof, while a huge lightweight hexagonal flysheet kept the rain off my single-season sleeping bag and the rest of our kit. Travelling light meant we now cooked our meals on open fires and would forage for palm hearts, wild tomatoes and Brazil nuts as we went. At each camp one of the team would be tasked with catching fish using our two gill nets, or with baited hooks on wire leaders that the piranha couldn't bite through.

In August 2008, I was joined by Gadiel 'Cho' Sanchez Rivera, an Afro-Peruvian forestry worker, who initially agreed to act as my guide for five days, but ended up sticking with me for the next 733. Despite some close encounters with deadly spiders and snakes, the biggest dangers in the Peruvian jungle actually came from people; we were pushed about by half-drunk officials, threatened by distrustful locals, and were always on the lookout

for the gun-toting drug runners. In one village we were held at gunpoint on suspicion of murder. But the scariest encounter came in early September 2008, when we were ambushed in the river by a group of highly agitated Asheninka people, charging at us in half a dozen dugout canoes, brandishing shotguns and arrows. These were hairy moments and I was glad to have my stalwart companion, Cho, at my side.

Like Tim Slessor in his First Overland adventure through Burma (now Myanmar), I had decided against carrying my own firearm, which could be easily misinterpreted as a sign of aggression – the episode with the Asheninkas could have turned out very differently if I had been armed with a rifle. My only protection, if the worse were to happen, was my Ralph Martindale 45cm (18in) machete; a lovely piece of kit, sharpened to a razor's edge.

January 2009 marked the beginning of the wet season and the waters were beginning to rise. As the waters rose, the banks of the Amazon spilled into the jungle, creating vast stretches of várzeas

(flooded forest). We had to 'handrail' the river, often tens of kilometres into the jungle, in order to find dry land. Inside my rucksack was an Ortleib 100 litre (22 gallon) waterproof rucksack liner that did a fantastic job of keeping all our kit dry. Semi-inflated it also kept me buoyant in the water and took the pack's weight off my shoulders. To keep our guides' kit dry, and cross rivers when we needed to, we also carried two inflatable packrafts, and strapped to the sides of our rucksacks, four-piece carbon-fibre paddles.

The insects at this point were driving us insane, averaging ten bites a minute; which by my calculations meant around 4,800 mosquito and sandfly bites over a typical eight-hour trek. The DEET insect repellant was too precious to waste in the daytime, where sweat quickly washed it off, and was saved for lunch and rest stops.

On these long wet marches, looking after one's feet became a top priority. Every morning I would apply Vaseline to my feet before putting on my damp socks, and in the evening would wear Crocs around the camp to give them the chance to breathe and dry out. Last thing at night, by the light of my Petzl head torch curled up in my hammock, I would always give my feet one last look over for the warning signs of trenchfoot before dipping them into my 'foo foo' bag of medicated talc.

Another camp routine was to wash out clothes in a river or stream each night and hang them by the campfire to dry out. To save weight we only carried two sets of socks, a quick-drying t-shirt and

a pair of loose-fitting trekking trousers – I ditched the underwear early on; two layers of fabric just left you with a damp, spotty bum. My baseball cap was essential to keep the sun off my head and to swat away the relentless mosquitoes. Earlier on in the trip I had worn an expedition shirt, covered in sponsors' logos and impregnated with insect repelling permethrin; great for keeping the bugs off, but it made me look a little too much like a DEA (Drug Enforcement Administration) agent … not a good image in this part of the jungle.

While walking the Amazon I experimented with all sorts of footwear, but my trusty Altberg Jungle boots carried me for most of the way. Based on a US military design, they were comfortable and offered good protection from the thorny undergrowth. However, early on in the trip, I found their 'drain valves' would often clog up with silt from the river; the second pair I ordered were specially modified with free-draining eyelets on the instep – it's impossible to keep your feet completely dry in the jungle and this new design worked fantastically well.

In March 2009, with the Peruvian south bank of the Amazon flooded and impassable, we were forced to trek through a section of southern Colombia, despite the increased risk of encountering the drug cartels.

To stop family and friends worrying back home, and keep our supporters informed of our progress, I blogged about our adventures. Safely tucked away, in additional dry bags filled with silica gel sachets, we carried an Apple MacBook

Opposite The large waterproof rucksack liner inside my 90-litre (20-gallon) Macpac rucksack helped keep me bouyant when wading through the Amazon, and took some of the weight off my aching shoulders.

Below The Alpacka inflatable packrafts were perhaps the most important piece of equipment we carried on the expedition, transporting people and equipment across the Amazon and its tributaries.

EXPEDITIONS UNPACKED

with two spare batteries, two satellite phones and a Sony camcorder, which used DV cassette tapes that were couriered back to the UK from the bigger towns we passed through. However, constant damp and humidity meant that much of this high-tech equipment didn't survive for very long, and finding power to charge it all up became a constant problem. We did experiment with 2m (6ft) solar-charging mats, but under the dark rainforest canopy they didn't work well; instead, we had to carefully eke out the power each day until we reached civilisation.

In August 2009, we entered one of the most remote parts of the Brazilian rainforest, forging a 560km (350 mile) path across the meander bend that goes from Porto Seguro to Tefé. Living on strict rations and foraged forest food, we were burning around 4,000 calories more than we were consuming each day, and losing weight rapidly. When a troop of black caiman (relatives of the crocodile) ripped our fishing nets to shreds, Cho was forced to improvise, using our Leatherman multitool to turn a chain of sewing needles into a piranha-proof fishing rig; smoked over the campfire and dipped in salt, these vicious little blighters were absolutely delicious.

Deep in the jungle our GPS died. All we had to navigate by was the sun, a cheap Casio wristwatch, a 1:1,000,000 aeronautical chart and a plastic compass from the UK (which hadn't been balanced for use in South America where the Earth's magnetic field dips down).

The weeks we spent battling through these inhospitable swamplands, close to starvation and low on water, were some of the most exhilarating days of the entire expedition. Free of technology, we gained an insight into what it must have been like for early jungle explorers like Fawcett.

By December 2009, with twenty-one months behind us, but over seven still to go, morale was getting low. I tried to keep my mind active listening to Spanish and Portuguese language lessons on my iPod Nano, and by helping Cho to improve his English.

Thankfully, over those final few months, as news of my adventures began to spread, I was increasingly interacting with people via my blog. Using our BGAN satellite link I was able to answer direct questions from primary school children and geography students back in the UK, and even conduct the odd TV interview, which really lifted our spirits. I felt it was important that I used this opportunity to talk about the amazing places we'd seen, the fantastic people we had met, as well as the environmental devastation we had witnessed due to unsustainable deforestation and mineral exploitation.

Thanks to this final flurry of support, those final few months flew by. Until, on Monday, 9 August 2010, 860 days, 8,000km (5,000 miles), ten HD cameras, three GPSs and six pairs of Jungle boots after leaving the shores of Peru, Cho and I walked onto the sands of Maruda Beach amid a barrage of jostling reporters and cameramen's flashguns.

It was finally over: I had walked the Amazon from source to mouth to set a new Guinness World Record. I, too, just like my childhood heroes, had achieved something 'amazing' that I would forever be proud of.

Sarah Outen

_____

Born: 26 May 1985, UK

'What's next?' Like so many adventurers, this was the perennial question that Sarah Outen faced after becoming the youngest person, and first female, to row solo across the Indian Ocean in 2009. However, when asked by Prince Edward at a charity event, Outen, for the first time, talked about an idea she had been mulling over of: 'looping the planet using human power: rowing across the Pacific and Atlantic oceans, cycling across the continents in between and kayaking to join up the dots.' Now, having announced her London2London expedition plans to nods of royal approval, there would be no going back.

London2London Unpacked

Expedition:
Circumnavigation of the globe by rowing boat, bike and kayak

Date:
2011–2015

Length:
4.5 years

1. Ocean rowing boat
2. Neoprene peaked visor
3. Large yellow Peli case
4. Panniers
5. Cycling shoes
6. Aquapac dry bags
7. Iridium satellite phone
8. Laptop
9. Penknife
10. Parachute anchor
11. Trekking bike
12. GPS chart plotter, Automatic Identification System, VHF radio
13. Kayak
14. Paddle
15. Inflatable globe
16. Personal Locator Beacon
17. Survival suit
18. Union Jack flag
19. Custom rowing seat
20. Sunglasses
21. Maritime compass
22. Bike helmet
23. Sailing jacket
24. Buoyancy aids
25. Map
26. Glowsticks
27. Wind generator
28. Tent

EXPEDITIONS UNPACKED

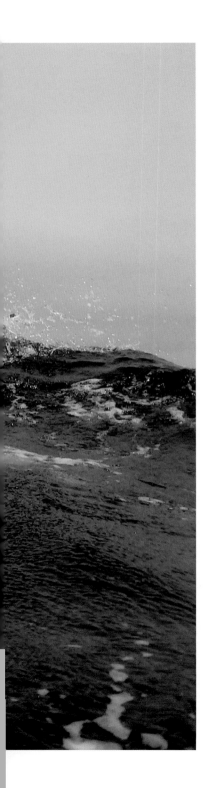

Less than two years after announcing her plan to circumnavigate the globe, using human power, on 1 April 2011, Sarah Outen paddled *Nelson*, her 5.2m (17ft) fibreglass kayak, down the River Thames and underneath the ornate ironwork of London's Tower Bridge, the official starting point of her 40,000km (25,000 mile) voyage around the northern hemisphere. Klaxons blared as well-wishers whooped and waved from the decks of the two escort vessels as they made their way downstream with the ebbing tide into the flat lands of Essex and Kent.

On this first leg, Outen was accompanied by her sea-kayaking team-mate, Justine Curgenven, carrying tents and provisions for the three-day paddle to France.

Built by Rockpool in North Wales, Outen's sea kayak was one of the first to feature a raised knee feature for a more comfortable sitting position over long distances, and was especially suited for choppy sea crossings.

At 10.30 p.m. on the third day, the pair began the eight-hour night time paddle across the English Channel, the busiest shipping lane in the world, with glowsticks attached to their buoyancy aids and a well-lit escort vessel watching for traffic. Navigating by the small maritime compass mounted in front of the cockpit, the cranes of the Port of Calais loomed out of the morning mist marking the start of the long cycling leg east.

Essential kit carried aboard *Nelson* was transferred to the five black panniers mounted on *Hercules*, Outen's heavy-duty trekking bike built by the Dutch company Santos. Painted gloss black and fitted with a Brooks leather saddle for comfort, the aluminium bike featured a hub with fourteen internal gears, driven by a composite belt rather than a chain, which required no lubrication and was virtually maintenance-free.

Donning her helmet, sunglasses and clipping her cleated cycling shoes into her pedals, Outen pushed off from the French coast threading a path eastwards along miles of well-marked and well-maintained cycle lanes through Belgium, the Netherlands and into Germany, sharing her route with pedalling locals on shopping bikes, commuting schoolchildren and Lycra-clad wannabe racers.

At the start of her journey, Outen preferred to use a simple paper map, which gave a better sense of geography. She stashed this in the top of her handlebar bag along with her donated Mars bars and an iPod loaded with motivational tunes. However, anxious to reach eastern Russia in time to make the pre-winter crossing to Japan, Outen 'traded prettiness for pace' sticking to fast major roads through Eastern Europe, and clocking up to 145km (90 miles) per day.

Much of the time Outen camped wild. When kindly locals offered her a warm meal or shelter for the night she would try to explain the enormity of

Below *Hercules* with bulging panniers
stands guard beside Sarah's tent
whilst wild camping at 2,100m (6,890ft)
in rural China.

EXPEDITIONS UNPACKED

the journey with the aid of an inflatable globe that she carried in her pannier. Back home, supporters were kept up to date on her progress via her regular blog posts and tweets from her Iridium satellite phone and modem.

Roads began to deteriorate rapidly after Outen crossed the Russian steppe into Kazakhstan, with friendly truckers shouting a concerned 'nyet doroga' (no road) to Outen as she bucked along eastwards. *Hercules* had solid steel forks, rather than the usual suspension setup of modern mountain bikes. However, the frame's geometry did allow clearance for off-road tyres. With better grip, but higher rolling resistance, Outen became a slower moving target for stray dogs, which she repelled with squirts from her water bottles, and vicious mosquitos.

Thankfully, relief appeared every 80km (50 miles) or so along Kazakhstan's dusty potholed roads in the form of 'chai kanurs' – shabby transport cafés, selling cheap and calorie-packed bowls of plov, made with camel meat and rice, stodgy naan breads and boiled dumplings, which made a welcome change to the pasta and dehydrated meals Outen could boil up on her small camping stove.

In July 2011, Outen arrived in China. Lingering at a petrol station snack bar to savour the cooling blast of its air conditioning, she was approached by a young man named Gao yua Guang who was enthusiastic to know more about Outen's adventures. On a whim, Guang asked if he could join her on the five-week, 4,800km (3,000 mile) leg to Beijing. Outen gave him a long equipment list and scary stories of the hardships ahead, believing she would never see him again. Two days later, just as she had finished chopping her hair into a crude bob with her trusty penknife, a similarly shorn-headed Guang arrived at her hotel in Lycra cycling gear on a shiny new bike loaded with camping equipment.

Within a couple of days the pair hit the searing heat of the Gobi Desert and began cycling at night by the light of *Hercules'* dynamo-driven headlamp to escape the 45°C (113°F) midday sun. Outen was impressed by Guang's can-do attitude and spirit of adventure, the very thing she hoped to inspire in others through her London2London expedition.

'I knew that Gao was scared and that the ride would be challenging … but by saying the words out loud and committing to having a go, Gao had overcome the biggest obstacle in his way.'

Above Measuring just under 7m (23ft) long, *Gulliver* was constructed from a Kevlar reinforced skin over a lightweight foam sandwich. Solar panels provided the power for all electrical items, including a desalination unit for turning saltwater into fresh.

After crossing back into Russia, Outen was reunited with *Nelson* and her kayaking buddy, Curgenven, for the 1,600km (1,000 mile) paddle and pedal to Japan, via the remote Russian island of Sakhalin.

As winter set in, the tent's ice-covered flysheet would crack like glass as it was unzipped each morning. To keep out the cold, Outen now layered up with merino wool garments beneath her Gore-Tex cycling jacket. Made from the wool of New Zealand's mountain sheep, the renewable high-performance fabric isn't itchy or bulky like the woollen sweaters worn by Captain Scott's men, or flammable and prone to body odour like the synthetic materials pioneered by Reinhold Messner and his ilk in the 1970s. Only Outen's hands and feet really suffered from the damp and cold on the tough ride across Sakhalin, forcing her to improvise with plastic food bags inserted into her cycling shoes and Aquapac dry bags over her gloves for extra insulation.

After a tough 50km (30 mile) paddle across the La Perouse Strait, Outen landed on the Japanese island of Hokkaido in early October 2011. Making her way south by both bike and kayak to the island of Honshu, she spent the winter months recuperating and preparing *Gulliver*, her 7m (23ft) custom-built rowing boat, for the 7,250km (4,500 mile) row across the north Pacific. Constructed from a Kevlar-reinforced skin over a lightweight fibreglass and foam sandwich, *Gulliver* had three main parts: a front cabin for storage, a rear one where Outen slept and the electronics were housed, and a rowing seat mounted on Rollerblade wheels on the open deck in the middle. Capable of carrying one tonne of cargo, there were enough provisions aboard to survive six months at sea.

On 13 May 2012, Outen rowed away from Choshi Marina south-east of Tokyo. For the first three weeks, despite the choppy conditions, she made good progress as a powerful arm of the Kuroshio Current pushed *Gulliver* eastwards.

Above Wearing her drysuit and bouyancy aid, Outen drags Nelson onto the black sand beach of Chikhachyova Bay in eastern Russia.

Left Outen passes below a snow-capped volcano during her 1,600-km (1,000-mile) paddle from Russia to Japan in the autumn of 2011.

Right View from inside *Happy Socks*, showing Outen's sleeping arrangements, map on the ceiling and photographs of friends and family. Scrawled on the cabin walls were motivational quotes and good luck messages from her supporters.

However, all that was to change on 6 June 2011 sea as Typhoon Mawar hit and 15m (50ft) waves began to pound the tiny boat. Outen stowed her oars, shackled the 4m (13ft) wide sea anchor to the bow and threw it into the sea and deployed the red and yellow Ocean Safety parachute, which would hopefully prevent the boat from turning broadside into the waves and so reduce the risk of capsizing. She herself retreated to the rear cabin, strapped herself into her narrow sleeping bunk with her four-point chest harness and leg loop restraints, to ride out the storm.

Every hour Outen sent brief texts from her satellite phone to let folks know she was OK. 'As the barometer plummeted and winds became shrieking harpies, waves a seething, tumultuous mess, the brevity of my messages belied my fear.'

With winds gusting to 130km/h (80mph), *Gulliver* repeatedly capsized, ripping off radio antenna and carbon-fibre safety rails, and jamming the rudder; inside the cabin, clothes, drinking bottles and the large yellow case containing camera gear clattered off the cabin's ceiling and walls

as seals failed and footlockers began to fill with seawater. After rolling over more than twenty times, with shorting electronics and damaged steering gear, Outen had no choice but to activitate her Personal Locator Beacon to await rescue by the Japanese Coast Guard as she shivered in her sodden cabin, wrapped in her red survival suit and a Union Jack flag for warmth.

Repatriated to the UK, Outen was unsure whether she would ever complete her London2London expedition after the trauma of Typhoon Mawar and the irreparable damage to her rowing boat. And then, that autumn, Outen received a call from her boatbuilder to let her know that *Gulliver*'s sister ship was up for sale. With support from sponsors and family, the winter became a whirlwind of activity preparing the newly rechristened *Happy Socks* for a second attempt.

Outen rowed out from Choshi Harbour, on 27 April 2012, bound for Canada. Four months later, as the easterly ocean currents petered out and the weather deteriorated, Outen decided to land at Adak, in the Aleutian Islands. Paddling *Krissy*

(a three-piece kayak built for easy transportation) eastwards along the archipelago, Outen stepped ashore in Homer, Alaska, after 251 days on the water. Glad to be on dry land, she was reunited with her sturdy 14-speed steed, *Hercules*, for the next leg across North America.

Cycling through one of the worst winters ever recorded, it took Outen seven months to reach the Atlantic coast at Cape Cod, Massachusetts, to prepare for the long row back to England. To supplement the solar panels fitted to the cabin roofs, *Happy Socks* had been fitted out with an additional wind generator to help power the numerous electronic gadgets: communication equipment, GPS, VHF radio, as well as the desalinisation unit (capable of producing 25 litres (5½ gallons) of fresh drinking water every hour) and the waterproof speakers mounted on deck.

Rowing solo for four months across the North Atlantic Ocean, Outen had been making good progress until, just 1,600km (1,000 miles) from the Irish coast, *Happy Socks* was hit by Hurricane Joaquin. Supporters onshore predicted that

conditions would be even worse than those she had experienced in the Pacific in 2012; the tough call to abandon ship was made, and within a couple of hours Outen was picked up by a passing ship.

Determined to bring the London2London expedition full circle regardless, Outen set off on *Hercules* from Falmouth harbour amid a peloton of friends, family and supporters towards Oxford in October 2015. Returning to the water for the final kayak down the Thames, Outen paddled *Krissy* under London's Tower Bridge on 3 November 2015, four and a half years after setting off. As horns blared, crowds cheered and the Thames fire boat sprayed its water canons, Outen swung between tears and laughter during the emotional finale to her epic adventure.

'I was coming home with so many new things. Treasured memories of the miles beneath my boats and my wheels … A faith in the goodness of people and a deeper respect for nature.' This was a journey that tested Outen to her absolute limits: 'and was, in many respects, all the richer for not turning out exactly as planned.'

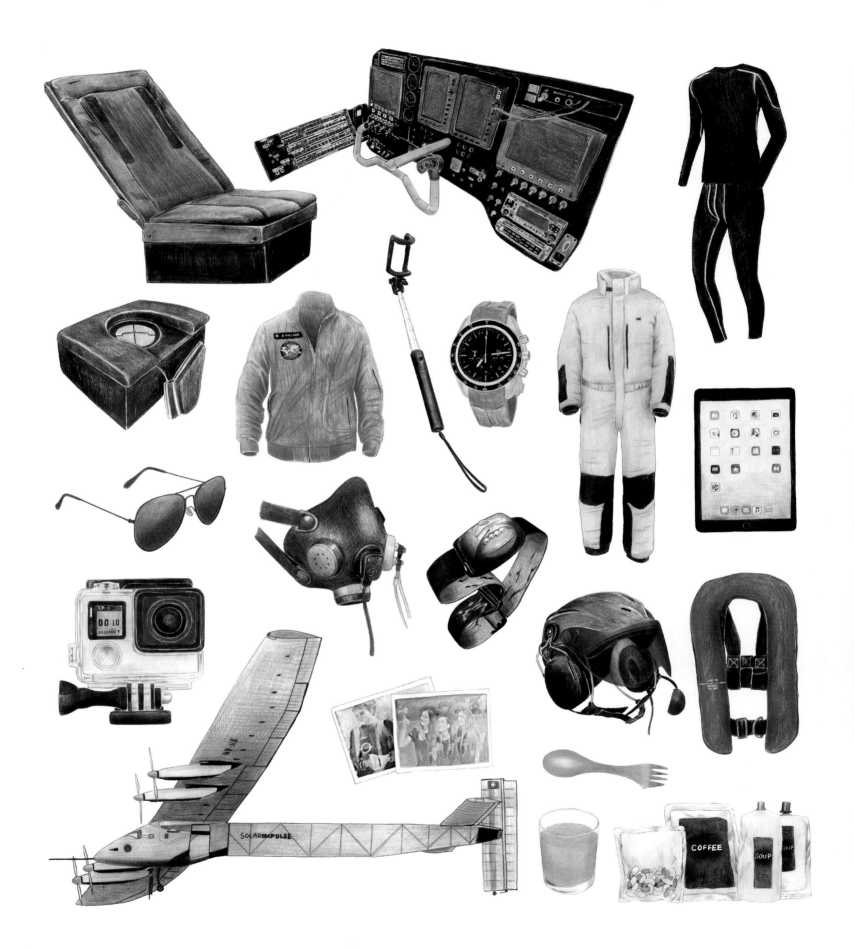

Bertrand Piccard & André Borschberg

Bertrand Piccard born: 1 March 1958, Switzerland
André Borschberg born: 13 December 1952, Switzerland

In 1999, Swiss adventurer Bertrand Piccard became one of the first men to fly non-stop around the world, as the co-pilot of the *Breitling Orbiter 3*. This 55m-tall (180ft) hybrid balloon was lifted partly by helium and partly by hot air, warmed by six propane burners for which 3.7 tonnes of liquid propane was carried aboard. When he landed in Egypt, after the 20-day voyage, just 40kg (90lb) of propane remained. 'I made a promise that the next time I flew around the world, it would be independent from fossil energies.' In June 2016, with his partner, André Borschberg, he fulfilled that promise.

Flight Round the Globe Unpacked

Expedition:
First around-the-world solar-powered flight

Date:
2015–2016

Length:
16 months (in stages)

1. Fully reclining seat
2. Cockpit controls
3. Base layers
4. Toilet
5. Jacket
6. Selfie stick
7. Omega watch
8. Flight suit
9. iPad
10. Aviator glasses
11. Oxygen mask
12. Head torch
13. Helmet
14. Safety harness
15. GoPro camera
16. Solar Impulse 2
17. Photos of family
18. Spork
19. Orange juice
20. Food supplies

EXPEDITIONS UNPACKED

Left Bertrand Piccard flies *Solar Impulse 2* over San Fransisco's Golden Gate Bridge in April 2016.

Experimental remote-controlled solar-powered aircraft, with 4m (13ft) wingspans, had already demonstrated that the battery technology existed to allow non-stop flight, day and night. But Bertrand Piccard and **André Borschberg** knew that if they wanted the public to change their perceptions about solar-powered air travel, and to embrace the idea of a fossil-fuel-free future, then they needed to embark on a 'human adventure' with pilots who could engage with universities, inspire students and talk to politicians.

Gathering a specialist team of sixty-five scientists and engineers, they set up a project headquarters in Lausanne in 2007 and started construction of a prototype solar-powered aircraft, capable of a manned flight.

In December 2009, *Solar Impulse 1* made its maiden flight, powered entirely by energy harnessed from photovoltaic cells that covered the top of the aircraft's wings and tail. This powered four twin-bladed propellers, which delivered about the same horsepower (over an average 24-hour cycle) as the Wright brothers' *Flyer* of 1903, the world's first heavier-than-air aircraft.

Just seven months later, the plane took off from Payerne Air Base in Switzerland for a record-breaking 26-hour test flight, using the potential energy of gained height and stored battery power to keep it aloft throughout the night.

Having demonstrated that night-time solar-powered flight was entirely possible, construction began on a larger and more powerful aircraft that would be capable of carrying a pilot, and all the equipment and provisions necessary, for a trip around the globe. Bearing the Swiss registration code HB-SIB, *Solar Impulse 2* had a wingspan of 71.9m (236ft), slightly more than a Boeing 747 airliner. However, unlike the 400-tonne Jumbo Jet, this aircraft, constructed from a lightweight carbon-fibre honeycomb, weighed just 2.3 tonnes – less than a new Range Rover.

On 9 March 2015, after exhibiting *Solar Impulse 2* at the World Future Energy Summit in Abu Dhabi, 63-year-old former Air Force fighter pilot Borschberg took off on the first 772km (480 mile) leg to Muscat in Oman. The original plan was to circumnavigate the globe entirely within the northern hemisphere, over twelve legs between March and August 2015, with the two Swiss pilots alternating at each stopover.

Piccard took the 1,593km (990 mile) second leg from Muscat to Ahmedabad in India. Reaching

a height of 8,874m (29,114ft), the aircraft could cruise at 50–100km/h (30-60mph) during the day. Above 3,600m (12,000ft) the air becomes too thin to meet the body's needs and the pilots had to rely on supplemental oxygen. To reduce weight the two men used anti-hair-growth creams, rather than the heavier shaving kit, to keep their stubble at bay and maintain a good airtight seal with the oxygen mask. As *Solar Impulse 2* climbed above the clouds, the sun's UV rays also became more intense and high-altitude sun creams were applied to the skin, while dark-lensed aviator glasses and helmet visors protected the pilots' eyes from the glare.

At maximum altitude, the temperature inside the unheated cabin could drop to -20°C (-4°F). To keep warm the pilots wore modern wicking base layers, and specially designed underwear that stimulated blood circulation, beneath their high-tech flight suits. Made of 'intelligent' nylon fibres, the suits maintained body temperatures with inflated air pockets and by directing infra-red heat back to the skin's surface. However, as the daytime cabin temperature could soar to 35°C (95°F), the suits also avoided the problem of excessive perspiration with a series of vents and openings. In extremely cold conditions additional down-filled layers could be added, and electrically heated insoles and gloves activated to keep extremities warm. Nevertheless, changing clothes was a pretty arduous task, as the pilots were not allowed to remove their safety harness (connected to a parachute and life vest) at any time during the flight.

Below *Solar Impulse 2* flies over the Red Sea during the last leg of its record-breaking circumnavigation. Its four 17.5hp motors gave the solar-powered aircraft a top speed of just 140km/h (87mph).

BERTRAND PICCARD & ANDRÉ BORSCHBERG

Despite several weeks' delay due to strong headwinds, *Solar Impulse 2* finally completed its crossing of Asia, landing in Nagoya, Japan, on 31 May 2015. Here, the team waited for a break in the weather to begin the longest stage of the team's circumnavigation: the 8,924km (5,545 mile) crossing of the Pacific Ocean to Hawaii.

On 28 June 2015 mission control, based in Monaco, gave Borschberg the green light for the five-day flight nicknamed the 'Earhart Leg' after the ill-fated American aviator who disappeared while crossing this same desolate expanse of water seventy-seven years earlier in her Lockheed Electra.

'It's going to be the moment of truth,' Borschberg told reporters in Japan. 'To demonstrate to the world that solar-powered aircraft can fly indefinitely throughout the day and night without landing, or using a single drop of fossil fuel.'

After seven hours he passed the point of no return, since he was now reliant on the available daylight hours to ascend to high altitude while recharging the aircraft's lithium-ion batteries, before throttling back the motors and slowly descending to 914m (3,000ft), drawing as little current as possible from the battery reserves, during the hours of darkness.

During the flight Borschberg kept his mind active by filming life inside the cockpit with his GoPro camera and vlogging from his Apple iPad. To promote good blood circulation, and avoid life-threatening clots, he practised a specially designed yoga and pilates programme from his cockpit seat. By reclining the seat flat, the pilots were able to take regular 20-minute naps, while the aircraft's autopilot took care of essential functions. If the alarms on their Omega Speedmaster wristwatches failed to wake them up, or the plane encountered difficulties while they slept, flashing lights in the pilot's goggles and vibration pads in the sleeve of the flight suit (also developed by the Swiss watchmaker) would rouse them.

When *Solar Impulse 2* landed at Honolulu on 3 July 2015, after 117 hours and 52 minutes airborne, it set a new world record for the longest solar-powered flight, by both time and distance. However, during the flight the large 633kg (1,395lb) batteries, which had been encased in too much insulation, had overheated and become badly damaged. By the time the new parts were sourced and fitted, it was too late in the season, with insufficient daylight hours to make the next long hop across the Pacific to the US mainland.

Grounded until the following spring, Piccard retook the controls for the three-day flight to California on 21 April 2016. During the journey he was able to address Ban Ki-Moon before the General Assembly of the United Nations, via video link, to discuss the potential environmental and economic benefits of clean energy technology. Over the entire journey the pilots would conduct thirty live interviews using their onboard iPad, receive 25 million likes on Facebook and 12,106 questions set by visitors to the Solar Impulse website. Predictably, the most common question posed by schoolchildren was: 'How do you go to the toilet?' Bertrand answered this question in his video diary, removing a small access panel from the pilot's seat to reveal the hidden commode below, admitting that answering the call of nature while gazing out of the cockpit windows at high altitude over the ocean was a 'very Zen experience'.

After flying across the USA, via Arizona, Oklahoma and Pennsylvania, Piccard took off from New York on 20 June for the 71-hour transatlantic crossing to Seville, Spain. On these long, tiring journeys over the featureless oceans, mealtimes became the highlight of the day, and the nutritionists at Nestlé Research put 6,000 man-hours into developing tailor-made meal plans for each pilot that were appetising, nutritious and calorie-dense to help cope with the cold at high elevations. Nestlé also recognised that the pilots' nutritional needs

varied with altitude and designed foods to be eaten at different times of the day: below 3,500m (11,500ft), meals were in bigger portions and richer in protein, while foods eaten later in the day as they reached higher altitudes required higher levels of fat and carbohydrate.

Readymade soups, curries and risottos were vacuum-sealed in compact pouches, designed to avoid spillage, which were either self-heating or warmed up in a small 'hot box' located towards the rear of the cockpit. Despite space and weight restrictions, a few treats were carried aboard to help keep up morale, including bars of Cailler (Switzerland's oldest chocolate brand), dried fruit snacks and instant coffee.

Borschberg's last flight was the penultimate leg across Europe, flying over the Mediterranean Sea and the pyramids at Giza, before landing in Cairo. During his time aboard *Solar Impulse 2*, he set ten new world records. However, it was Piccard, the

man who had conceived the idea for a flight round the world using only energy harnessed from the sun, who had the honour of flying the final 48-hour stint back to Al Bateen Executive Airport in Abu Dhabi. Touching down just before midnight on 26 July 2016, eleven months later than originally planned, *Solar Impulse 2* became the first solar-powered aircraft to circumnavigate the globe after 558 hours and z7 minutes of flight time, covering 42,438km (26,370 miles) at an average speed of just 76km/h (47mph).

Solar Impulse 2 had achieved what, just ten years earlier, many had believed was technically impossible. While most people still doubt that we will see solar-powered passenger planes any time soon, it is worth remembering that when Charles Lindbergh flew across the Atlantic for the very first time, he too was pushing his aircraft to its absolute limits. Yet less than fifty-years later, Concorde, the world's first supersonic passenger airliner, would be crossing the Atlantic in just three hours.

Above A cyclist aboard a Swiss-made Stromer electric bicycle helps guide the pilot onto the runway during a night landing at Muscat, Oman.

Left Piccard, wearing his 'intellegent' flight suit, celebrates after a gruelling three-day flight from Hawaii to Moffett Airfield in California's Silicon Valley.

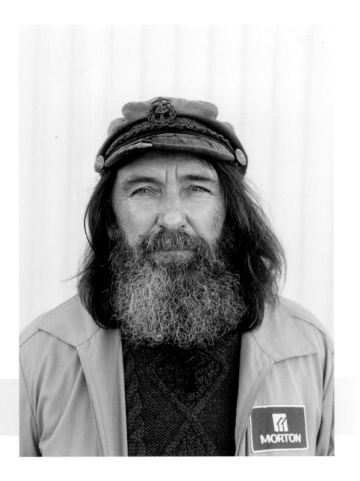

Fedor Konyukhov

Born: 12 December 1951, Ukraine

Fedor Konyukhov embarked on his first major adventure when he was just fifteen years old, rowing across the Sea of Asov in a fishing boat. Over the next five decades he set world records for rowing across the Atlantic and the Pacific; he was the first to circumnavigate Antarctica by sailboat and the third to complete the Explorers Grand Slam, reaching both Poles and climbing the highest mountain on each continent. Having completed almost every physical challenge the land and oceans could throw at him, in 2016 the 64-year-old artist, author and ordained Orthodox priest decided to take to the skies.

Transglobal Balloon Flight Unpacked

Expedition:
Fastest round-the-world balloon flight

Date:
2016

Length:
11 days

1. Gondola
2. Russian flag
3. Head torch
4. Hot-air balloon
5. Kit bag
6. Down suit
7. Champagne
8. Marine radio
9. Thermos flask
10. Depiction of Saint Nicholas
11. Duct tape
12. Mariner's cap
13. Helmet
14. Rucksack
15. iPad
16. Satellite phone
17. Sleeping bag
18. Stopwatch
19. Laptop
20. WD-40
21. Spoon
22. Depiction of Virgin Mary
23. Oxygen regulator
24. Hard case
25. Glasses
26. Wrench
27. Autopilot
28. Wallet
29. Camera
30. Flight instrument deck

There had been twenty-nine attempts to circumnavigate the Earth by balloon before 2016, but only two of them had been successful: Bertrand Piccard and Brian Jones did it first in 1999 in the *Breitling Orbiter 3*, and the American aviator, Steve Fossett, flying solo aboard the *Spirit of Freedom*, set a record time in 2002 of 13 days, 8 hours and 33 minutes. Both balloons had used a combination of hot air and helium for their uplift, and had been constructed by the specialist balloon company Cameron Balloons based in Bristol, England. With a global reputation as experts in this field, Fedor Konyukhov approached them to build him an aircraft, declaring: 'Nobody in the world makes better balloons than the Brits.'

Known as a Rozière balloon, the hybrid design contained two separate chambers for the lighter-than-air helium gas and an envelope for hot air below. The advantage of this design for extended flights was that there was no need to carry cumbersome sandbags as ballast, which you would normally have to jettison at sundown to slow your descent. Instead, the propane burners used small amounts of fuel to heat the air and helium to stabilise its height during the night, making it far more efficient than a traditional hot-air balloon.

Bearing the name of his key sponsor, Konyukhov's *Morton* was made of a lightweight insulating material. It was 33m (108ft) wide – the width of two double-decker buses parked end to end – and as tall as Italy's leaning tower of Pisa, at almost 59m (194ft) high. Beneath the fireproof strip of fabric at the base of the balloon were six propane burners, connected to thirty-four stainless steel cylinders strapped the gondola's sides, providing enough fuel to last up to twenty days.

Made of lightweight carbon fibre, the bright yellow gondola measured just 2 square metres (21½ square feet). The only window to the outside world was an acrylic observation dome on the top. Featuring a watertight hatch and two keels on the bottom, the gondola could act as a lifeboat in the event of an unplanned splash down.

Konyukhov had hoped to start his voyage in Russia. However, to catch the best possible weather, and utilise the high-altitude jet-stream currents, it was decided to launch from Northam in Western Australia (the same place that the *Spirit of Freedom* had taken off from) sometime between June and August 2016. By starting the flight during the southern hemisphere's winter, it reduced the risk of tropical storms and cyclones, or the helium cells overheating.

FEDOR KONYUKHOV

EXPEDITIONS UNPACKED

Left Konyukhov's 59m (194ft) high British-made Rozière balloon, used a combination of helium gas and hot air heated by six propane burners to keep it aloft for up to 20 days.

The cruising altitude for Konyukhov's flight was envisaged to be somewhere between 5,000–8,000m (16,400–26,250ft) above sea level, roughly the same heights as Everest Base Camp and the beginning of the Death Zone just below the summit. Having climbed Everest twice before, with the use of supplemental oxygen, the Russian adventurer returned to the Himalayas two weeks prior to the provisional launch date to acclimatise his body to the rarified air he would be experiencing in his unpressurised balloon capsule.

After several postponements caused by delayed equipment and bad weather, a launch window was finally set and frantic last-minute preparations were made. Under the watchful eye of the British flight director, it took thirty local volunteers an entire day to lay out the 1,600kg (3,530lb) balloon. Wearing his trademark mariner's cap Konyukhov checked last-minute items including his ration packs, the first aid kit, his Canon camera and emergency repair kit, including duct tape, wrenches and cans of penetrating oil and water-displacement spray, which would be needed to stop gas valves from freezing and seizing up.

Anchored to a Toyota pickup truck, *Morton* was half-filled with helium in the early hours of 12 July 2016. As it took off, and slowly ascended, the air pressure decreased and the heat of the morning sun began to warm the helium chambers, and the balloon began to expand. When the small Russian flag on top of the gondola stopped fluttering, Konyukhov knew that *Morton* had reached its cruising altitude and was matching the airspeed of the powerful easterly jet stream.

Heading over the Tasman Sea, Konyukhov had to try and steer his way towards New Zealand by ascending and descending to pick up the most appropriate currents. Generally, winds veer clockwise the higher you go, but they can vary by ninety degrees or more in lower altitudes. As an experienced sailor (having circumnavigated the globe via Cape

Horn four times), Konyukhov was able to read the clouds, avoiding unstable air masses and the worst weather as much as possible, and finding the most favourable currents to whisk *Morton* eastwards at speeds of up to 300km/h (190mph).

Conditions on that first day were almost perfect, and Konyukhov quickly settled into a busy routine of navigation tasks, reading instruments, calculating fuel consumption and changing tanks, as well as preparing meals and grabbing short naps of thirty to forty-five minutes, nestled in his thick down sleeping bag on the cabin's narrow bunk. During this much-needed rest a special on-board Comstock Autopilot maintained the balloon at a constant altitude by using a computer to control the burners.

However, much of the equipment on board *Morton* was experimental and had never been fully tested in these kinds of extremes. On day four, the gas canister for the heating and cooking stove exploded, depriving Konyukhov of any way of preparing his freeze-dried meals and sending the cabin temperature plunging. Exiting the gondola, he found a way to periodically divert propane away from a small navigational burner for the stove, which helped a little, but for the remainder of the voyage Konyukhov was still unable to get the cabin temperature above -20°C (-4°F). As water supplies on board froze he had to resort to putting ice scraped from the gondola's sides into a metal kettle and holding it next to the burners with a stick to thaw it out, saving what he could in his Thermos flask to ration throughout the day.

He was now reliant on supplemental oxygen for his brain to function properly, since at 8,000m (26,250ft) the air only contains a third of the oxygen it has at sea level. In the freezing cabin he had to deal with the constant irritation of his oxygen regulator and mask icing up.

To make matters worse, on day five, at 8,500m (27,890ft) above the Pacific, Konyukhov noticed that his oxygen cylinder was faulty. To avoid

suffocation, he had to climb onto the top of the gondola and adjust a valve to stop the oxygen escaping.

The cold and damp began to make the sensitive electronic navigation and communication equipment malfunction. While he had to brush the hoar frost off his flight instrument deck, he tucked his Iridium satellite phone inside his thick down-filled Red Fox flight suit to make sure he could always maintain contact with his ground crew.

On the night of 18 July 2016, *Morton* encountered strong turbulence. Konyukhov exited the gondola and by the light of his Petzl headlamp began dropping half-empty bottles of propane so the balloon could ascend to calmer weather above 8,200m (26,900ft). During these challenging hours he had to keep a constant eye on his instruments and be on the lookout for cumulonimbus clouds, which signalled bad weather.

In a state of constant alert he was unable to sleep, allowing himself only a few seconds' rest at a time using a technique he had learned from the Russian military: holding a spoon between two fingers he would close his eyes momentarily until the clang of the dropped cutlery would rouse him again. 'I couldn't sleep, not even for a minute,' he said. 'If I had dozed off, I would have fallen.'

Cold, sleep-deprived, dehydrated and painfully hungry, Konyukhov still faced one last major hurdle on the final leg back to Australia. A huge storm had gathered over the Indian Ocean, and his chief meteorologist in Belgium realised that there was no way around it – the only option was to face it head-on. For three hours lightning flashed around Konyukhov, threatening to send him plummeting into the ocean, as he fought to find calmer weather at higher altitudes. In communications with his ground team, he reported that, at this point, he was in 'survival mode'.

The deeply religious adventurer believed that disaster had been averted through prayer and the help of the sacred objects that he had brought with him: a Virgin Mary icon painted for him by Orthodox monks, a framed depiction of Saint Nicholas, the patron saint of sailors and, fixed to one wall of his cabin, a large silver cross said to contain the relics of forty-six saints.

Eventually finding more stable air in the polar jet stream at 10,614m (34,823ft), the cabin temperatures dropped to -30°C (-22°F). Konyukhov had inadvertently set a new world record for the highest altitude ever achieved by a balloon, but this strong high-level air current began to take him perilously close to the Antarctic Circle,

Above Fedor sits at *Morton*'s flight instrument deck wearing his famous mariner's cap. On the rear of his seat are the Willans harness straps used to secure himself during his landing in Australia.

where he could spot icebergs out of the observation window in the seas below. Blogging from his laptop he wrote that it was: 'scary to be so down south and away from civilisation. This place feels very lonely and remote. No land, no planes, no ships.'

Relief finally came on the eleventh day as he spotted the west coast of Australia through the observation dome, and realised that Steve Fossett's record was now within his grasp. Pursued by six helicopters and several Toyota pickups on the ground, *Morton* passed over the Northam airstrip it had taken off from, but flew on for another hour. Eventually, the gondola thumped down on a cattle ranch, bouncing over the empty fields before tipping onto its side and being dragged along for several hundred metres. Finally, one of the pursuit crew got their Toyota's tyre over the tether that trailed

behind the gondola and it came to a standstill. Badly shaken up, Konyukhov was helped from the gondola, wearing his protective yellow helmet and sporting a bloodied cheek from his bumpy landing. He was greeted by emotional family and friends with a bottle of champagne in the time-honoured ballooning tradition. Severely dehydrated and almost 11kg (24lb) lighter due to the faulty cooker, the one thing Konyukhov now craved more than anything was sleep.

The 64-year-old Russian priest had spent a perilous 269 hours and 11 minutes cooped up in a freezing cabin little bigger than a double bed, and beaten Fossett's fourteen-year-old record by more than two and a half days. Few balloonists think that this feat will ever be bettered and even fewer would risk trying.

Olly Hicks & George Bullard

Olly Hicks born: 4 November 1982, UK
George Bullard born: 7 April 1989, UK

In 1728, a dying man washed ashore in a craft made from sealskins, driftwood and whalebone, close to the village of Belhevie near Aberdeen. He wasn't the first such visitor and locals called them 'Finnmen' because they thought they had come from Finalnd. However, artefacts in this man's kayak suggested he was an Inuit hunter from Greenland. Was it humanly possible that this man could have paddled 1,930km (1,200 miles) across the treacherous North Atlantic Ocean? Intrigued by this 300-year-old mystery, two British adventurers, Olly Hicks and George Bullard, set out to test the theory.

Voyage of the Finnmen Unpacked

Expedition:
Greenland to Scotland by kayak

Date:
2016

Length:
65 days

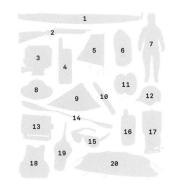

1. Sea kayak	14. Carbon-fibre paddles
2. Rifle	15. Sunglasses
3. GoPro camera	16. Satellite tracker
4. Satellite phone	17. Gas stove
5. Sails	18. Flotation device
6. Inflatable pontoons	19. EPIRB rescue beacon
7. Drysuits	20. Tent
8. Compass	
9. Waterproof tents for the kayak	
10. Para-flares	
11. Fishing line	
12. Baseball caps	
13. AIS transponder	

EXPEDITIONS UNPACKED

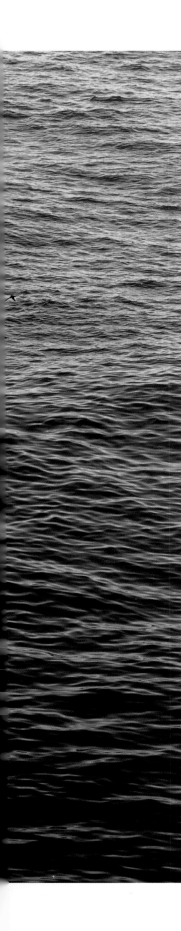

Described as the 'Arctic Kon-Tiki', the Voyage of the Finnmen expedition began on 1 July 2016, launching from a support vessel, as close to the Greenland coastline as the pack ice would allow.

However, unlike Thor Heyerdahl's famous balsawood raft, Olly Hicks and George Bullard were in a two-man sea kayak made of high-tech carbon fibre with a reinforced Kevlar hull. Measuring 6.8m (22ft) long, the *Unik Duo* was specifically designed for long-distance unsupported expeditions, capable of carrying 100kg (220lb) of gear within its four watertight hatches, and had bungee cords on deck for lashing down dry bags and other smaller items. Despite the boat's reputation as a rough water model, kayaks are not ideal for multi-day open-ocean expeditions, as they are more prone to capsize than other types of boat and are only fully stable when moving forward at speed.

Threading through the Greenland ice floes, Hicks and Bullard had to keep a keen eye out for predatory polar bears, keeping their cut-down Ruger .45-70 rifle close at hand. Fortunately, once they were out in open water, the sea conditions for the first day's paddle were almost perfect: with a gentle wind behind them, the two men were able to make good use of the kayak's two triangular sails; a technology that was similarly employed by the Inuit in their open-decked Umiak whaling boats.

After 18 hours, and over 65,000 strokes of their carbon-fibre paddles, the two men had made good progress, making it almost half-way across the black polar waters of the Denmark Strait before resting up for the night.

Burning around 4,000 calories a day, it was vitally important for the men to refuel each evening with a hot, calorie-dense meal to stave of hypothermia. To try and stabilise the boat, as they heated their ration packs on a small gas stove precariously wedged between their knees, four inflatable pontoons were lashed to the boat's sides. Unlike the Inuit aboard the Belhevie kayak, the two paddlers were able to slide down below the cockpits into small sleeping compartments with a waterproof tent that zipped over the top. To further reduce the chance of capsize, a sea anchor was deployed to keep the kayak pointing into the waves. For Hicks, this small fabric parachute was the most useful piece of equipment they carried; Bullard later claimed that the one bit of kit he would advise any long-distance kayaker to carry with them was a good-sized pee bottle.

At this latitude in the summer, the sun barely sets, and after just six hours' kip the two began the second day's paddle southeast towards Iceland. Under the bright Arctic skies, they kept the sun's glare out of their eyes with iridescent Oakley sunglasses and black baseball caps bearing their key sponsor's logo. The wind that had pushed them onwards on the first day was now whipping up the sea and crashing waves across the deck.

The biggest risk to their survival was keeping warm and dry as they crossed these frigid polar seas. While the Inuit made watertight clothing from whale and seal intestine, Hicks and Bullard sported drysuits made from triple-layer Gore-Tex with latex collar and cuffs to keep out the elements. Over the top they wore matching personal flotation devices, with their multiple pockets bulging with snacks and repair gear, including Sugru moldable glue, patches, cable ties and their Leatherman multitools.

Navigating by the illuminated maritime compass mounted in front of the rear cockpit, it was hard to gauge how fast the kayak was moving with no visual frames of reference. For Bullard, as a novice kayaker, this became quite demoralising at times. Hicks, however, was a much more experienced maritime explorer: in 2005 he had been the youngest person to row solo across the Atlantic. Keeping faith in their instruments, and thanks to their high levels of physical fitness, they sighted the north Icelandic coast after just 50 hours of paddling, almost a day ahead of schedule. Landing on the remote black sand beach at Hornvik they quickly set up camp, chopping up driftwood with 'Betsy', their trusty straight-bladed machete, to build a blazing campfire.

Their tent was described by Hicks as a 'wonderful home away from home, and an absolute palace compared to sleeping in a kayak'. Aboard the boat the two wore cumbersome neoprene coats (originally developed for kitesurfers) over the top of their Gore-Tex drysuits, to try and keep warm as they slept. Now on land, Hicks slipped on his favourite Buffalo jacket, relishing the chance to nestle into his down-filled sleeping bag – an 'old friend' that had accompanied him on all his adventures 'from the Sahara to the Antarctic'.

The second stage of the expedition involved a 700km (440 mile) traverse of Iceland's rugged north coast, hopping between the towering headlands that guarded the entrances to its deep ice-carved fjords.

Buoyed up by their impressive start on the first leg, they launched off the beach the next morning and paddled off eastwards. However, as the waves began to grow, they quickly realised that they hadn't been as thorough as they should have been with their pre-launch weather checks. With a biting wind whipping the sea into 3.5m (12ft) waves, the two men realised that they were now in a 'paddle or die situation', knowing that the more tired they got, the less likely it was that they would have the strength to right a capsized canoe. Fighting against the foaming sea, it took them six terrifying hours before they reached the safety of a bay where they could safely land.

Huddled in a wooden seaman's refuge hut they sat out the storm. Hicks had brought a bottle of whisky for just such an occasion: 'To take the edge off a scary day at sea, when you've been taught once again how small and insignificant you are, and shouldn't be mucking about in Neptune's garden …'

Using their satellite tracker, which plotted the kayak's position, and the Iridium satellite phone to make contact with their support team, Hicks and Bullard began to make better use of the technology available and studied weather information more diligently. If the worse were to happen they carried aboard the kayak emergency para-flares, an EPIRB (emergency position-indicating rescue beacon) and an AIS (automatic identification system) transponder that alerted shipping in the vicinity to their whereabouts. Nevertheless, if they did capsize, and were unable to right the boat, it was unlikely that any help would arrive in time to save them.

Opposite top Hicks and Bullard wearing triple-layer Gore-Tex Kokatat Expedition Drysuits with msFIT Tour personal flotation devices.

Opposite bottom Hicks and Bullard silhouetted against the night's sky after landing in the Faroes.

Above Hicks and Bullard inspect their maps. In the background their Kaitum 3GT tent was an 'absolute palace' compared to sleeping in the kayak.

Back in the confines of the kayak's cockpit after a two-day wait for better weather, Bullard noted, with a wry smile: 'It's a weird feeling knowing that you're already sitting in your coffin!'

After a tough sixteen days, Hicks and Bullard were within sight of the final landing point on Iceland's east coast. Pausing in the sheltered inshore waters, Hicks used the GoPro camera mounted on the kayak's deck to update his video diary, while Bullard caught dinner on his handheld fishing line, hauling aboard a decent-sized Atlantic cod; running dangerously low on supplies, the fresh fish was a welcomed addition that night. In the event of an emergency, the two knew that they would have to live off the land to survive. As well as the fishing gear and the rifle, they also carried various knives, a froe for splitting kindling and a hand-powered watermaker similar to the one used by Jason Lewis on his human-powered circumnavigation.

Neskaupstaður on Iceland's east coast was to be the launch pad for the expedition's longest ocean crossing: the 480km (300 mile) journey to the Faroe Islands, through a perilous stretch of water

nicknamed the Devil's Dancefloor due its dangerous currents and violent winds. Hicks and Bullard needed a six-day weather window to get safely across, but the forecasts were only accurate for the next three. After a two-day wait they 'rolled the dice' and began paddling southeast towards the Faroe Islands.

While the seas were fairly calm, after two days a thick fog enveloped the kayak, adding to the sense of isolation that the two men already felt. On the third day, as the fog began to lift, they were spotted by the *Audur Vestiens*, a 15m (50ft) Icelandic longliner. The captain couldn't believe what these 'crazy guys' were doing in the open ocean. Didn't they know that hurricane-strength winds were forecast for this region that evening?

Despite losing three days of paddling, Hicks and Bullard took up the captain's offer of a lift back to Iceland; he was convinced that they would not have survived had they pushed on towards the Faroe Islands. Over the next six days, as they waited for a break in the weather, they repaid the captain's kindness working on the fishing vessel, setting out 16,000 hooks on 16km (10 miles) of

Below Made of carbon fibre with a reinforced Kevlar hull, the Unik Duo sea kayak was designed for long-distance unsupported expeditions and could carry 100kg (220lb) of equipment stowed within its four watertight hatches or lashed to bungies on deck.

line, and bringing in the catch to the fishing village of Stodvarfjordur.

On the seventh day the weather broke, and after a slap-up breakfast in the fisherman's café they headed out of the fjord under a clear blue sky. This time, the weather was kind and progress was good. They landed on the Faroes in a tranquil sheltered bay at 3.00 a.m. on the fourth day of a crossing that they thought would take six.

By now it was late in the summer; the days were getting shorter and the prevailing weather was about to turn against them. After waiting for almost three weeks in the little fishing village of Porkeri, a small weather window opened up. They had just 48 hours to make the 290km (180 mile) dash for the mainland before conditions turned ugly again.

On paper, this should have been an easy home run. However, after a weather and navigation check late on the second day, they realised that they were not going to make Scotland before things dramatically worsened, and they headed for cover on the uninhabited island of Rona.

For the next six days, gale-force winds blasted the rocky outcrop as they sheltered in an abandoned scientist's shelter on the west side of the island, using their free time to scavenge for limpets and hunt for seabirds to eek out their dwindling food rations.

Eventually a message came through on the Yellowbrick tracker to say that the gale was due to subside and they should prepare for the final 80km (50 mile) home leg. Well rested and filled with confidence now that the finish line was within grasp, the two men paddled hard. With just 16km (10 miles) to go they could smell the mainland.

Accompanied by a pod of dolphins and the bobbing navigation beacons of nearby trawlers, they headed towards the blinking light of the Cape Wrath lighthouse. As dawn broke on 4 September 2016, the spectacular Sutherland coastline came into view; where, on the small sandy beach of Balnakeil Bay, friends and family had already gathered to welcome the two adventurers home.

After five years in the planning, Hicks and Bullard had achieved what they set out to do. Much like the Kon-Tiki expedition of almost seventy years earlier, it wouldn't completely rewrite the history books, but it did add weight to the romantic idea that 300 years ago Inuit seafarers paddled their sealskin kayaks 1,930km (1,200 miles) into the unknown, to pioneer new routes linking northern Europe to the Arctic Circle.

Apa Sherpa

Born: 20 January 1960, Nepal

Ever since the 1920s, when the first climbers attempted to ascend Mount Everest, they have been assisted by Sherpa guides and mountain porters from the surrounding area. Between 1953 and 2018, there have been 8,306 successful summits of Mount Everest by 4,833 different people. Around half of those summits were by Sherpa guides, many of whom have reached the top multiple times. Perhaps the most admired serial summiteer is Apa Sherpa, the Nepalese mountaineer who, in May 2011, topped the 8,848m (29,029ft) peak for a (then) record-breaking twenty-first time.

Everest Unpacked

Expedition:
21 Everest ascents

Date:
Various

Length:
Various

1. Mountaineering suit	14. Energy gels and drinks
2. Waterproof rucksack	15. Steel crampons
3. Summit oxygen system	16. Tent
4. Dehydrated food	17. Ice axe
5. Parabolic solar cookers	18. Ultraviolet Steri Pen
6. Goggles	water purifiers
7. Ice anchors	19. Mobile phone
8. Solar-powered lighting	20. Heated socks
9. Goose down sleeping bag	
10. Aluminium ladders	
11. nylon rope	
12. Climbing boots	
13. Gore-Tex and goose down gloves	

EXPEDITIONS UNPACKED

As a boy Lhakpa Tenzing Sherpa – or 'Apa' dreamed of becoming a doctor, walking six hours every day to attend the Himalayan Trust School that had been set up by Sir Edmund Hillary in the 1960s. However, when his father died suddenly, Apa was forced to abandon his studies to work as a trekking porter to support his family. In 1985, he joined his first mountaineering expedition, and first reached the summit of Everest in 1990, alongside Peter Hillary, son of Sir Edmund Hillary. Over the next two decades Apa joined a string of expeditions, impressing clients from across the globe with his ability to carry huge loads and his sunny disposition.

As one of Nepal's most experienced mountain guides, Apa witnessed the rapid commercialisation of the Everest region when the first professional guiding companies began taking paying clients, known as 'members', up the mountain in the 1990s. When Apa first summited with Peter Hillary, less than 400 people had stood on the 'roof of the world'. On 19 May 2012, 234 climbers reached the summit on a single day, some queuing for two hours for their turn on the top. In 2018, the most successful season on record, over 800 mountaineers summited Everest.

Despite its increasing popularity, climbing Mount Everest is still a serious undertaking, fraught with dangers. To date, an estimated 290 people have died climbing Everest; the majority still lying on the mountain where they fell. Despite their genetic adaptations to life in this oxygen-starved environment, around one third of these fatalities have been Sherpas. While statistically they comprise the largest group on the mountain, they are also the most exposed to its risks, making up to forty passes through the notorious Khumbu Icefall each season, setting up equipment and carrying supplies. The bravest Sherpas of all are the 'Icefall Doctors' who forge the paths and place aluminium ladders across dangerous crevasses, secured with ice anchors and screws. Every year, the climbing Sherpas set out 10,000m (33,000ft) of fixed nylon rope along the South Col route to guide members to the summit.

While an experienced Sherpa can earn up to $10,000 a year, roughly ten times the average Nepali wage, their chances of being killed on the job are more than ten times higher than a US soldier serving in Iraq. But despite its grisly reputation, it is considerably safer to climb Mount Everest today than it was when Reinhold Messner was breaking records in the 1970s and 1980s – with the death rate dropping from around one fatality per seven successful summits to around one in sixty since the year 2000. The reduction in casualties is primarily down to better equipment, more reliable weather forecasts and an increasing number of professional high-altitude guides being hired to assist expeditions.

Apa's carbon-fibre ice axe is a good example of how technology has moved on since Hillary first hacked his way through virgin snow to the summit of Everest with his heavy forged-steel and ash-handled ice axe. Lighter equipment means faster ascents, reduced fatigue, fewer accidents and less time spent in the Death Zone. Climbers on that 1953 expedition carried their equipment in old army rucksacks weighing 20kg (44lb) apiece. Today's ultralight gear, carried in a modern waterproof rucksack, might cut that payload by half.

During his twenty-one summits Apa saw footwear technology rapidly improve. Before Messner pioneered the first plastic climbing boots in 1978, frostbite had claimed, on average, at least one toe of every other Everest summiteer. Modern boots are even better insulated and feature integrated gaiters and snug heat-mouldable liners. For mountaineers that really feel the cold, a company called Hotronics has even developed a range of electrically heated insoles and socks, which have been successfully used on many of the world's highest mountains.

Climbers on the 1953 expedition already appreciated the insulating qualities of down-filled jackets, with the first one-piece climbing suit being used on Everest in 1971. Modern-day mountaineering suits use the finest goose down insulation, topped off with a breathable outer layer that's capable of withstanding temperatures down to -50°C (-58°F), but weighs just 1.4kg (3lb). Similarly, modern goose down sleeping bags offer excellent insulation properties, and a waterproof outer layer, at just a third of the weight of Hillary's bag.

The cotton-nylon A-framed assault tents of the 1950s have long been superseded by modern geodesic yurts. The North Face VE 25 has been a favourite of many Everest climbers for nearly twenty years, and is a home from home that Apa became very familiar with. Designed to withstand fierce winds and temperatures down to -60°C (-76°F), it weighs a third less than the Mead tent used by Hillary on the night before the big push.

Since Messner first climbed Everest without supplemental oxygen in 1978, fewer than 200 others have managed the same feat. While Hillary relied on a crude open-circuit system weighing more than 8kg (17lb) (with a single cylinder fitted), the latest systems weigh less than half that. They are also more compact and offer a more reliable and controllable flow of oxygen.

As well as better and lighter equipment, improvements in weather forecasting have also contributed to the increasing number of successful summits and the reduction in casualties on Everest. When Apa summited for the seventh time via the Southeast Ridge in 1995, weather predictions were made by observations on the mountain and gut instinct. But after the disaster in 1996, when eight climbers were killed in a blizzard that had blindsided them on their descent, guiding companies began to recruit professional meteorologists who used satellite imagery and other weather data to make accurate three-day forecasts.

When Apa returned to Everest as a Sirdar (lead Sherpa) with an Indonesian expedition in 1997, most parties were using satellite phones to receive weather updates on devices about the size of a large laptop. Today you can get a 4G signal on top of Everest allowing smartphones to receive hourly weather updates, as well as broadcasting your location and uploading summit selfies straight to your social media.

However, one of the biggest changes on Everest has been the rise in the number of Sherpas hired by the commercial operators. In 1992, when Apa supported a New Zealand expedition, there were, on average, around five members per Sherpa. Today it's closer to two, allowing less experienced climbers to offload gear and carry more oxygen. Having a Sherpa cook on your team is also especially helpful when you are burning 10,000 calories per day. Fuelling the body in the Death Zone above 8,000m (26,247ft) is not an easy task: most climbers lose their appetite, and digestive systems shut down, just when the body needs it most. While Hillary wolfed down a tin of sardines, some apricots and a few dried biscuits back in 1953, modern-day climbers carry calorie-dense dehydrated ration packs and energy gels to ensure they don't fail on the final push for the summit.

As Apa's reputation grew he earned the nickname 'Super Sherpa', due to the apparent ease with which he scaled Everest. To him the great Himalayan mountains are sacred, with Mount Everest at the centre as the 'Mother of the World'. In fact, many Sherpa consider it disrespectful for summiteers to stand right on the top, since that is where Miyolangsangma, the Tibetan 'Goddess of Inexhaustible Giving', sits.

While Apa and his Sherpa colleagues rely on the income provided by the trekking parties and sport climbers who visit the region each season, the environmental toll that decades of commercial expeditions have had on their revered mountain has been horrific. Ripped tents, food packaging, empty

gas cylinders and tonnes of human excrement now litter the main routes up towards the summit.

Since 2008, Apa has supported the annual Eco Everest Expeditions, which have made huge steps to clean up Everest and highlight how climate change has impacted on the region. In 2011, when Apa completed his twenty-first and final ascent of Mount Everest, the group brought 13.5 tonnes of rubbish, 400kg (882lb) of human waste and the wreckage of a crashed Italian helicopter down to base camp to be recycled and disposed of. In 2017, the clean-up operation recovered a whopping 25 tonnes of trash and 15 tonnes of human waste – enough to fill three double-decker buses. Thanks to the Eco Everest Expeditions, Apa and his team were also able to field test and promote an array of sustainable mountaineering technology, including parabolic solar cookers, solar-powered lighting and ultraviolet Steri Pen water purifiers.

In a recent interview Apa explained that: 'When I first climbed Everest there was a lot of snow and ice, but now most of it has become rock. That, as a result, is causing more rockfalls, which is a danger to the climbers.' With less snow for climbers to dig their steel crampons into, accidents are more likely,

and climate change could be behind movements in the Khumbu Icefall, such as the house-sized block of ice that broke free in 2014 causing an avalanche that killed sixteen climbing Sherpas.

In May 2018, 48-year-old Kami Rita Sherpa climbed Mount Everest for the twenty-second time, beating Apa's long-standing record. While such achievements might bring fame and wealth to a small band of elite mountain guides, Apa has famously said that it's a profession that 'he wouldn't wish upon anybody'. Born into poverty he had no choice – something that he hopes to change for the next generation of Nepalese children through his work with the Apa Sherpa Foundation.

Set up in 2010, the foundation's mission is to increase the range of career options for young people in the Khumbu Valley region where Apa grew up. The foundation provides hot meals and teachers' salaries, and pupils are now able to attend school for 228 days a year. In 2013, in recognition of Apa's commitment to humanitarian projects and environmental conservation in the Himalayas, he was awarded an honorary doctorate from the University of Utah, USA, where he now lives with his wife and three children.

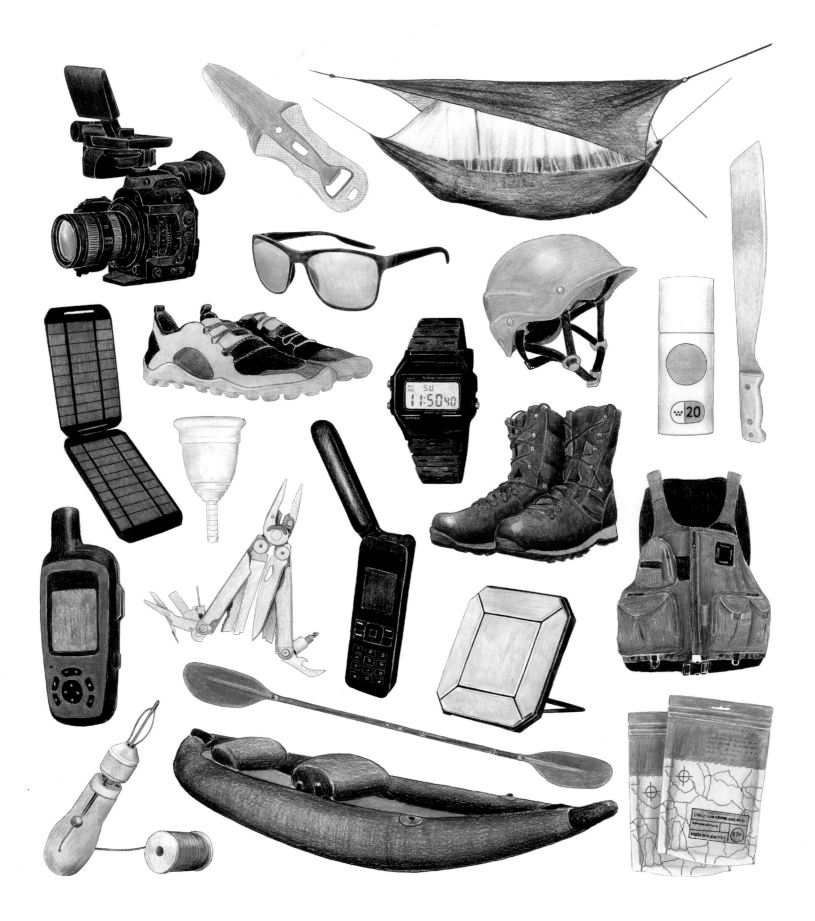

Laura Bingham

Born: 21 February 1993, UK

Rising in the Acarai Mountains in southern Guyana, the Essequibo River flows towards the north for 1,000km (630 miles). What starts as a stream in pristine virgin rainforest becomes a mighty 20km (12 mile) wide estuary as it empties into the Atlantic Ocean. Even though it is South America's third-longest river, no previous expedition before had ever succeeded in canoeing its entire length, from the source to the sea. In February 2018, a team of three female adventurers, led by the British explorer Laura Bingham, set out to become the first.

Running the Essequibo Unpacked

Expedition:
Caoneing the Essequibo from source to sea

Date:
2018

Length:
72 days

1. Canon cine camera
2. Knife in sheath
3. Sunglasses
4. Hammock
5. Helmet
6. Suncream
7. Machete
8. Powertraveller solar panels
9. 'Amphibious shoes'
10. Mooncup
11. Casio watch
12. Altberg Jungle boots
13. Garmin GPS and phone
14. Leatherman multitool
15. Inmarsat satellite phone
16. BGAN (broadband)
17. Flotation device
18. Speedy Stitcher sewing awl
19. Inflatable kayak
20. Two- or three-part paddle
21. Dehydrated meals

In August 2007, I had flown to Guyana to work as a Jungle Base Manager for the BBC Natural History Unit making a programme called *Lost Land of the Jaguar*. It was a stopgap job after leaving the Army, and a way to raise funds for my own jungle adventure, walking the length of the Amazon. Yet, the raw beauty of the forests, and the friendliness of the indigenous people, had such a profound effect on me, that I was still gushing about it a decade later. As Laura Bingham, my wife, recalls: 'Ed spoke about its beauty, the richness of wildlife, and its Disney-like landscape. He then mentioned that it was absolutely bonkers that no one had actually descended the river, source to mouth. This was the light bulb moment.'

Although Bingham had gained her sea legs crewing an 11m (36ft) trimaran across the Atlantic in 2014, like her fellow team members, Ness Knight and Phillipa Stewart, she had little kayaking experience. Knight had joined Bingham on part of her 11,265km (7,000 mile) unsupported cycling challenge through South America in 2016, and signed up like a shot when she heard about the Essequibo trip. Presenter and journalist Stewart had recently returned from a 4,830km (3,000 mile) expedition through the forests of Brazil and Peru, so she knew the perils of the South American jungles.

Over a frantic six months, letters were fired off to government agencies, permissions were sought,

equipment sourced and sponsors secured. In the depths of the British midwinter, team building, survival skills and canoe training then began, with a bit of help from myself and the Leicestershire Outdoor Pursuits Centre.

On the bitterly cold, but relatively calm, waters of the English East Midlands and the River Dee in North Wales, Bingham and her team familiarised themselves with their new expedition equipment. Northwest River Supplies (NRS) had supplied the team with 3.7m (12ft 2in) long inflatable kayaks made of a tough, abrasion-resistant, PVC-coated polyester. The advantage of this design, versus a traditional fibreglass canoe, was that they could be deflated and transported around waterfalls, rapids and other obstacles the team were likely to encounter. Similarly, the two-part fibreglass paddles made portage far easier. Canoeing helmets, boating gloves and duffel bags were also supplied by NRS, as were the compact Co-Pilot knives. Lashed to their personal flotation devices these 15cm (6in) steel blades were close at hand to cut ropes or other entanglements, and featured a blunt rounded tip – a handy feature when travelling by inflatable kayak.

Safety was of paramount importance in the headwaters of the Essequibo; if anyone needed to be evacuated by rescue helicopter then the team could trigger an SOS message and emergency beacon on their handheld satellite communicator

LAURA BINGHAM

Opposite With her equipment
stowed, kayak deflated and paddle
disassembled, Bingham prepares to
portage her gear around an obstacle.

and GPS tracker, but they would have to clear an area of rainforest the size of a football field so it could land. As Stewart noted in the expedition blog (typed up on my old Apple MacBook): 'We went into those upper regions knowing that if something happened, that would probably be it.'

In early February, after flying from the Guyanian capital Georgetown to the small airstrip near the Brazilian border, the team were warmly met by the indigenous Wai Wai people, whose lands the team would be travelling through. With the help of local guides, and with two cameramen in tow, the first challenge was to head upstream to seek out the source of the Essequibo River in the Wai Wai's dugout canoes. Heavy and cumbersome, with broad wooden paddles, they ploughed upstream as the tributaries became shallower and increasingly clogged with fallen trees, tangled vines and viciously spiny undergrowth that would have shredded the inflatable kayaks.

Heading ever upwards, Bingham and her team had to hack out a path using the 35cm (14in) steel machetes (my favourite piece of survival kit) that I had gifted to them as they left the UK. Climbing steep riverbanks, trudging through sucking-mud swamps and wading through bramble-choked streams made for very slow progress – they managed just 3km (2 miles) on their first day.

Making camp in the late afternoon, each would tie their lightweight hammock between the trees, under tarpaulins to keep off the rain. Covered with an ultra-fine mesh, the hammocks offered some much-needed sanctuary at the end of the day from the relentless biting insects, and protection from the various creatures that inhabited the forest floor. Over the next few weeks Bingham even perfected a way to pee out of hers – although when Stewart tried the same trick, it didn't go quite so well.

The best bit of advice I had for the team during this first phase of the expedition, based on my own experiences in the jungle, was to look after their feet. By the light of their Petzl head torches,

I encouraged them to check for damage each evening and dunk each foot into a 'foo foo' bag of medicated talc to reduce the risk of the dreaded trenchfoot.

Like myself, and Colonel Fawcett almost a century earlier, the greatest danger the team now faced was from jaguar, black caiman (relatives of the crocodile that can grow to 5m (16ft) in length) and a wicked assortment of spiders, scorpions and snakes. Although their sturdy Altberg Jungle boots offered some ankle protection, the team had been warned that a bite from Guyana's notorious labaria snake could be fatal within twenty minutes. These deadly pit vipers were mainly nocturnal, and certainly didn't appreciate being woken up. So when Stewart's boot crashed through a rotten log that a dozing labaria was hidden in, she narrowly missed being bitten on the backside with fatal consequences. 'Bushmaster, emorara and labaria – these are the three bad snakes of the jungle … pain, pain, pain,' warned their jungle guide.

It took Bingham's team three weeks, slogging up dozens of potential tributaries, until, 32km (20 miles) from the Brazilian border, they reached what is now officially acknowledged to be the furthest source of the Essequibo River. Gathering together in a cleft on the side of a thickly forested hill, the team logged the source's position using their GPS and recorded it for posterity using their cine camera.

After three weeks on foot, the nine-person team returned in the dugouts to the relative comforts of the Wai Wai village of Kanashan to prepare for the next stage of the expedition: paddling with the current towards the mouth of the Essequibo, 965km (600 miles) to the north.

Because the upper reaches of the Guyanese rainforest had never been filmed before, the team's cameramen had brought an arsenal of equipment to record as much of the landscape and wildlife as possible. In addition to the cine camera and various GoPro cameras they also brought two compact

EXPEDITIONS UNPACKED

drones, capable of shooting high-definition photos and video. Not only do these amazing gadgets capture some breathtaking aerial footage, but as I had discovered on my *Into The Unknown* TV series, they are also a brilliant expedition tool for surveying huge areas and spotting potential hazards that may lie ahead.

Out on the the river, the team quickly settled into a routine: rising before 6 a.m., the day would begin with a substantial breakfast, paddling until late afternoon when they would seek out a suitable camping spot for the night. These upper reaches of the Essequibo were idyllic, just as I'd described them to Bingham. As they progressed downstream, and the channel widened, the forest canopy opened up to reveal vivid blue skies and views of the unspoilt beauty of the Acarai mountain forests.

With the sun directly overhead at midday, waterproof sunblock, bush hats and dark sunglasses protected skin and eyes, but having permanently wet feet began to cause issues within days of leaving Kanashan. While Bingham and Knight wore free-draining Vivobarefoot Ultra III 'amphibious shoes' in the boats and around camp, Stewart's permanently sodden feet suffered a bad case of trenchfoot: 'Laura told me I looked like an 89-year-old about to die … my Instagram followers kept asking about "Boris". The infection was whitey-yellow and Boris seemed an appropriate name.'

In the calmer waters, the team were able to catch fish with gill nets and baited hooks to supplement their dehydrated meals and rations of rice, oats and lentils. More than 300 unique fish species have been discovered in the Essequibo including several varieties of piranha; these vicious little blighters will take your finger off if you don't handle them correctly, but smoked and salted they are absolutely delicious.

Prior to leaving the UK, the nutrition company Nuzest had taken blood samples and conducted DNA analysis of the team to fine tune their dietary requirements, supplying them with natural lean protein supplements for a low-carb, moderate-protein, high-fat diet – not that dissimilar to the pemmican staples of Roald Amundsen.

Obviously, water was plentiful and safe to drink in the upper reaches; but to be safe the team filtered their water through drinking bottles, which used carbon and iodine resin to remove viruses from contaminated sources. The small bottles of El Dorado rum the women carried for their evening nightcap probably didn't help with hydration, but it did help them sleep.

One of the expedition's objectives was to promote the concept of sustainable exploration and keep their ecological footprint as light as humanly possible. Food packaging was compostable; the team also operated a no-hunting policy within the surrounding jungle, and used the opportunity to field test the Mooncup – an eco-friendly alternative to traditional women's sanitary products that contribute to the global menace of single-use plastic pollution.

Six weeks into the expedition and the team were in good spirits, running well on a mix of bravado and black humour. However, physically, they were all beginning to suffer. All three were suffering with mosquito worms, more commonly known as botflies – irritating white lumps with larvae growing underneath. The best way to kill them is to suffocate them; in the Amazon I used superglue. Here on the Essequibo the Wai Wai improvised with strips of duct tape stuck to Stewart's shoulders and on Knight's and Bingham's bums.

Navigation downstream was done mostly on the fly using the preloaded maps and onscreen GPS routing on their Garmin satellite devices, which also contained built-in digital compasses, barometric altimeters and an accelerometer to help track their progress.

Other gadgets in their high-tech arsenal included their Inmarsat iSatPhone and BGAN portable satellite terminal that wirelessly connected

Above Bingham wades into the Essequibo to clear an obstruction using the 36cm (14in) steel machette I had gifted to the team before they left for Guyana.

Opposite Resting on a sandbar created by the wreckage of a crashed aircraft, the team uses its DJI Mavic drone to take some aerial photographs and survey the river ahead.

with the team's gadgets allowing them to receive weather updates or seek medical advice. To keep these electrical devices charged up the team also carried Powertraveller's solargorilla portable panels.

Ferrying their gear around the 15m (50ft) Kumaka Falls was a gruelling task in the humidity and heat of the midday sun. However, this marked the halfway point in their adventure and meant the toughest white-water canoeing was now behind them. But their relief was short-lived.

As they headed downstream they approached the first of many illegal gold-mining camps, observing the 'slow creep of humanity and civilisation', these camps brought different hazards to their wellbeing.

Cyanide and mercury-laden mining waste had devastated wildlife and indigenous communities along these river stretches, and the barren clear-felled moonscape allowed tonnes of topsoil to be washed into the Essequibo, clogging the channel

with unnatural sandbanks. The lack of sanitation for the thousands of miners that toiled here was also evident by the large human stool that floated by Knight's canoe. No longer able to drink directly from the river, the team would often have to approach the workers aboard the gold dredges to refill their water bottles.

After two months of paddling, the Essequibo had grown into a 20km (12 mile) wide estuary, dotted with dozens of low-lying islands. After 72 days and over 900km (600 miles), the final leg was into the face of a fierce headwind, through oil slicks and plastic waste – it couldn't have been a more dramatic contrast to the pristine upper reaches where the Wai Wai had first greeted them.

Nevertheless it was clear that nothing was going to dim the spirits of these three adventurers who, in their flotilla of inflatable kayaks, had paddled into the record books.

Index

Page numbers in *italic* type refer to pictures or their captions.

    EXPEDITIONS UNPACKED

Picture Credits

The publishers would like to thank the explorers, sponsors, picture libraries and photographers for their kind permission to reproduce the works featured in this book. Every effort has been made to trace all copyright holders but if any have been inadvertently overlooked, the publishers would be pleased to make the necessary arrangements at the first opportunity.

2-7 Herbert Ponting / Scott Polar Research Institute, University of Cambridge / Getty 8-9 Jonathon Williams 11 Keith Ducatel 12-13 Herbert Ponting / Scott Polar Research Institute, University of Cambridge / Getty 15 Science History Images / Alamy 17-19 l Bettmann / Getty 19 r Popperfoto / Getty 21 Age Fotostock / Alamy 22-27 l Herbert Ponting / Scott Polar Research Institute, University of Cambridge / Getty 27 r Herbert Ponting / Royal Geographical Society / Getty 28-29 Popperfoto / Getty 31 Bettmann / Getty 32-33 Library of Congress / Corbis / VCG / Getty 34 914 Collection / Alamy 35 Granger Historical Picture Archive / Alamy 36 Mondadori Portfolio / Getty 37 l Lordprice Collection / Alamy 37 r DeAgostini / Getty 39 Topical Press Agency / Hulton Archive / Getty 41 l M.L. Moennick / Royal Geographical Society / Getty 41 r P.H. Fawcett / Royal Geographical Society / Getty 42-45 Granger Historical Picture Archive / Alamy 47 IMS Vintage Photos 48-50 akg-images / TT News Agency / SVT 51 l Archive PL / Alamy 51 r IMS Vintage Photos 53 Klaus Niermann / Ullstein Bild / Getty 54-58 Taglichtmedia / Ullstein Bild / Getty 59 Ullstein Bild / Getty 61 IanDagnall Computing / Alamy 62-63 Bettmann / Getty 64 NC Collections / Alamy 65 Glasshouse Images / Alamy 66-67 Granger Historical Picture Archive / Alamy 69 CTK / Alamy 70-71 Everett Collection Historical / Alamy 72 TCD / Prod.DB / Alamy 73-77 The Kon-Tiki Museum 79 Everett Collection Historical / Alamy 80 OFF / AFP / Getty 82 l Everett Collection Inc / Alamy 82 r Granger Historical Picture Archive / Alamy 83 l George Rinhart / Corbis / Getty 83 r Paul Popper / Popperfoto / Getty 85 Keystone Press / Alamy 86 George Lowe / Royal Geographical Society / Getty 88-89 Alfred Gregory / Royal Geographical Society / Getty 90-91 George Lowe / Royal Geographical Society / Getty 92 Granger Historical Picture Archive / Alamy 93 Alfred Gregory / Royal Geographical Society / Getty 95-102 Jaguar Land Rover Limited 105 Hulton Archive / Getty 107-108 Ajax News & Feature Service / Alamy 109-110 Keystone Press / Alamy 111-112 Popperfoto / Getty 113 l Trinity Mirror / Mirrorpix / Alamy 113 r Keystone / Hulton Archive / Getty 115-125 Rick Smolan / Contour by Getty 126 Tim Roney / Radio Times / Getty 128-135 Scott Polar Research Institute, University of Cambridge 137 Franz E. Möller / Ullstein Bild / Getty 138-139 Nature Picture Library / Alamy 140-143 Messner Mountain Museum 145-153 Expedition 360 155-161 Alastair Humphreys 163-169 Rune Gjeldnes 171-173 Pete McBride 174-179 Keith Ducatel 181-189 Sarah Outen 191 Xinhua / Alamy 192-193 Jean Revillard / Getty 194-195 Jean Revillard / Solar Impulse 2 / Getty 196 Jean Revillard / Getty 198 Jean Revillard / Solar Impulse 2 / Getty 199 Jean Revillard / Getty 201-205 Fedor Konyukhov / Nikolay Ponomarev 206 Paul Kane / Getty 207 Fedor Konyukhov / Nikolay Ponomarev 209-212t Emma Hall 212b Niko Jager 214-217 Emma Hall 219 Apa Sherpa Foundation 220-221 Sameer Jung THAPA / AFG / Getty 222-223 Apa Sherpa Foundation 225-227 Jonathon Williams 229 Peiman Zekavat 230-231 Jonathon William 232 Peiman Zekavat 233 Jonathon Williams

Acknowledgements

A huge thank you to everyone who has worked so hard to make this book happen, including Jessica Axe, Emma Bastow, Christine Berrie, Isabel Eeles, Joe Hallsworth, Melissa Hookway, Julia Shone, Darryl Sleath, and Jess Stone, Laura Hill and Frankie Lyell at Independent Talent Group.

First published in 2019 by White Lion Publishing,
an imprint of The Quarto Group.
The Old Brewery, 6 Blundell Street
London, N7 9BH,
United Kingdom

T (0)20 7700 6700

www.QuartoKnows.com

A catalogue record for this book is available from the British Library.

ISBN 978 1 7813 1878 2

Ebook ISBN 978 1 7813 1879 9

10 9 8 7 6 5 4 3 2 1

Copy Writer	Darryl Sleath
Publisher	Jessica Axe
Comissioning Editor	Melissa Hookway
Editorial Director	Julia Shone
Project Editor	Emma Bastow
Copy Editor	Kath Stathers
Picture Researcher	Joe Hallsworth
Designer	Isabel Eeles
Production Controller	Robin Boothroyd

Printed in China